Proceedings of the

# FIFTH BIENNIAL INTERNATIONAL

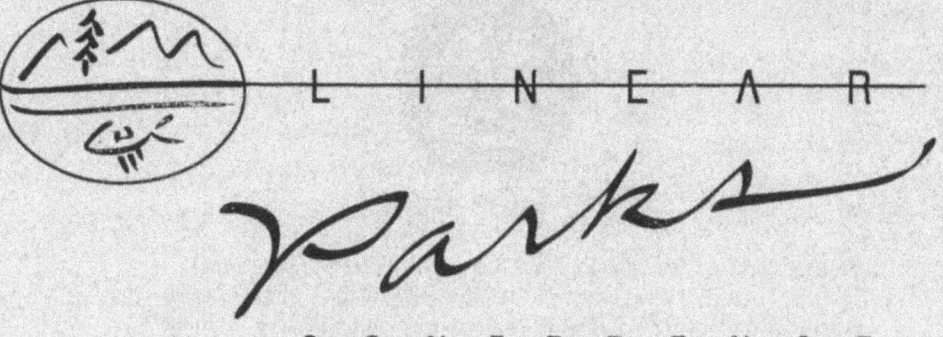

# CONFERENCE

September 8–11, 1993
Boone, North Carolina

*Marrying Beauty With Utility*

Appalachian Consortium Press
Boone, North Carolina 28608

The Appalachian Consortium was a non-profit educational organization composed of institutions and agencies located in Southern Appalachia. From 1973 to 2004, its members published pioneering works in Appalachian studies documenting the history and cultural heritage of the region. The Appalachian Consortium Press was the first publisher devoted solely to the region and many of the works it published remain seminal in the field to this day.

With funding from the Andrew W. Mellon Foundation and the National Endowment for the Humanities through the Humanities Open Book Program, Appalachian State University has published new paperback and open access digital editions of works from the Appalachian Consortium Press.

www.collections.library.appstate.edu/appconsortiumbooks

This work is licensed under a Creative Commons BY-NC-ND license. To view a copy of the license, visit http://creativecommons.org/licenses.

Original copyright © 1993 by the Appalachian Consortium Press.

ISBN (pbk.: alk. Paper): 978-1-4696-4248-2
ISBN (ebook): 978-1-4696-4249-9

Distributed by the University of North Carolina Press
www.uncpress.org

# 1993 Fifth Biennial International Linear Parks Conference

*Marrying Beauty With Utility*

# Contents

Keynote Address
    *Edward T. McMahon* .................................................4

The Urban Park of Oporto, Portugal
    *Sidónio Costa Pardal* ................................................8

Managing Change: The Blue Ridge Parkway as a Museum of
Managed American Countryside
    *Nancy K. Robinson* ................................................11

Beauty and Utility: Preserving the Urban Parkway
    *Peter S. Szabo* .....................................................22

Crisis in Viewshed Protection: Enlisting Community Support
    *Jim Fox* ............................................................28

Perceived Tourism Impacts and Attitudes Toward Land-Use Controls in
Communities Along the Blue Ridge Parkway
    *Sharon Kashkin and Gene Brothers* .................................34

Landscape Visibility Studies for a U.S. Forest Service Scenic Byway:
Mount Rogers National Recreation Area, Virginia
    *William E. Shepherd and Lynn Crafts* ..............................57

Protection of Scenic Resources Beyond Park Boundaries:
A Case Study from Roanoke County, Virginia
    *Janet Scheid* ......................................................68

Hope Diamond
    *Richard Posner* ...................................................72

The Public Spirit of the Recreation Demonstration Area Program
    *Bonj Szczygiel* .................................................. 76

Case Study: Devil's Courthouse Trail
    *Harry L. Baker* .................................................. 85

Evolution of Environmental Consciousness and Emergence of an
Environmentally Based Linear Parks Movement
    *William L. Flournoy, Jr.* ......................................... 90

The Historic Cultural Landscape and an Expanded Vision of Park
    *Thomas Yahner and Daniel Joseph Nadenicek* ....................... 96

Early Visions for a System of Connected Parks
    *Daniel Joseph Nadenicek* ......................................... 102

Managing the Blue Ridge Parkway Viewshed: A National Forest Perspective
    *Terry Seyden* .................................................... 110

Design and Construction of Park and Waterway Bridges
    *Eugene C. Figg, Jr.* ............................................. 113

The Appalachian Trail Crosses the Cumberland Valley (Abstract)
    *Neil P. Korostoff and Tom Yahner* ................................ 121

Congress and the Establishment of the John D. Rockefeller Jr.
Memorial Parkway, 1971-1972
    *Philip A. Grant, Jr.* ............................................ 122

Beauty and the Beast: Locational Logic of the Blue Ridge Parkway
    *Lisle S. Mitchell* ............................................... 125

# Keynote Address

*Edward T. McMahon*

Good evening! On behalf of the Conservation Fund and our President, Pat Noonan, I'd like to thank you for inviting me to speak at this 5th Biennial Linear Parks Conference.

The Conservation Fund is a national nonprofit organization committed to land and water conservation. Since our founding in 1986 we've saved over 400,000 acres of land, including wetlands, mountains, coastal islands, abandoned rail corridors and 25 Civil War sites. We work with partners and we seek entrepreneurial solutions to conservation problems. For example, we recently worked with International Paper Company to protect this 20,000 acre tract along the Racquette River in the Adirondack State Park.

The American Greenways Program, that I direct was established to help create a national network of linked natural areas and open spaces—greenways. In partnership with business, government, and nonprofit organizations, we act as a catalyst and a clearinghouse for linear parks and greenways at the national and state levels.

Aldo Leopold once said, "Everything is connected to everything else." Today I would like to talk about linear parks, greenways and some of the connections between conservation and economic development and between environmental protection and our quality of life, people and land.

About 20 years ago in a book entitled, *The Quiet Crisis and the Next Generation*, Stewart Udall said something that is more true today than ever. He wrote,

> America today stands on a pinnacle of wealth and power, yet we live in a land of vanishing beauty, of increasing ugliness, of shrinking open space, of an overall environment diminished daily by noise, pollution and blight.

Don't get me wrong. Over the past 20 years conservationists have made great strides. We've passed new laws to clean up air pollution, water pollution and toxic waste. To encourage recycling and energy conservation and to protect wetlands, sand dunes and other critical environmental areas. We've set aside millions of acres of land in parks and preserves and added thousands of buildings to the National Register of Historic Places.

But despite the gains the special character of America's cities and countryside is disappearing faster than ever. While we've been saving landmarks we've been losing our landscape. While we've been cleaning up air and water pollution we've been losing our sense of place. The truth is the American landscape is getting uglier, more fragmented and disorienting by the day.

Today a person suddenly air dropped along a road outside of any American city wouldn't know where he is because it all looks the same. Is it Albany or Allentown, Providence or Pittsburgh? Who can tell?

Rampant, unplanned growth severs our connections with a place, our essential orientations, ours sense of roots. As Wallace Stegner once said, "If you don't know where you are, you don't know who you are." We need points of reference and orientation. We need a sense of community, and a sense of place.

More and more people feel a growing dissatisfaction with the quality of *new* development. For all the improvements in environmental quality people still ask: Is this all there is? Can't we do better? Can't our communities be more *distinctive*?

*Marrying Beauty With Utility*

More *livable*? More *beautiful*? Can't we have more connection with nature and the outdoors?

Victoria Tschnikel, the former secretary of Environmental Regulation for the state of Florida, put it this way:

> I think we can probably take care of pollution-related problems in this state. But, even if we do, I'm not sure this is going to be a very nice place to live because of the density of population and the lack of sense of community. Florida could end up as just one convenience store after another.

Growth is inevitable. The destruction of community character and natural resources that so often accompanies growth is not. Progress does not demand degraded surroundings. We can grow without destroying the things people love. The real question is not whether our communities will grow but how. The failure to accept this is what causes many people to regard all development as the enemy. This fosters polarization and will defeat efforts to create a successful community.

The problem is not development, but rather the patterns of development.

- Where do you put it?
- What does it look like?
- What is the impact on natural systems and cultural landscapes?

North Carolina will not retain its special qualities by accident. Without exception, those places in this country that have successfully protected their uniqueness—whether natural, or man-made are those places that have used *vision*, and planning, to protect their special characteristics. To work a community's vision must accommodate change and development as well as environmental protection. As President Clinton has said, *The Invisible Hand of Adam Smith Can Have a Green Thumb!*

Unfortunately many people think we only have two development choices in America. The first choice they believe, is to buy land and to lock it up forever in a park or preserve, and the second is to allow unfettered, environmentally destructive, anything goes development right next door. These are not the only choices. We have a third choice. We can have growth and development that respects the character of a place and compliments the quality of the landscape. Development can be planned with new awareness of the economic and social values, of natural areas, open spaces, historic sites, scenic views and native plants and animals. North Carolina has tools to grow without destroying things people love—but it takes citizen action and political will to put these tools to work.

## NATURAL AREAS

We obviously need to continue to emphasize ecology and the health of natural systems. We need a whole ecosystem approach to restoring America's great water bodies and natural areas—like the Great Smoky Mountains, the Chesapeake Bay and the Florida Everglades.

We need to increase the amount of land devoted to habitat protection and to increase our scientific database so we know when we've accomplished our goals.

We also need a more holistic vision for the land. This brings us to linear parks and greenways.

Greenways are of course, not new. Frederick Law Olmsted coined the phrase "parkway" in 1865. Benton McKay proposed the Appalachian Trail—in 1921 and construction on the Blue Ridge Parkway—one of the world's most outstanding linear parks—began in 1935. Long popular in Europe, the many possibilities of these corridors is now attracting widespread attention across the U.S.

Greenways typically follow *linear landscape features:* watercourses, ridgelines, country roads, urban waterfronts, abandoned railroad lines, utility corridors, and other linear features.

- They can be as wide as a watershed or
- As narrow as a trail
- They can be publicly owned or established on private land with the understanding that it is limited to a trail easement or to protecting a stream or a vista.

Greenways do not look at one parcel or even one use. The goal is nothing less than a *network of green*—linking people, parks, historic sites and natural areas.

Greenways can provide a multitude of benefits for people, wildlife and the economy.

More expansive and flexible than traditional parks. They can provide a kind of community trail system for the linear forms of outdoor recreation Americans are engaged in today.

- jogging
- hiking
- biking
- boating
- horseback riding
- cross country skiing
- just plain strolling

## ENVIRONMENTAL PROTECTION

However greenways are *not limited* to *recreation*. They can provide:

- *lifelines for wildlife* moving from one isolated natural area to another.
- *preserve* biodiversity by protecting environmentally sensitive lands between protected areas.
- *protect water quality* by providing a buffer against runoff and non-point source pollution.

- *soften and direct* urban growth
- Act as an outdoor classroom where children can learn about nature. They can also provide pathways for people commuting to and from work.

—Louis Harris Poll

Greenways can also stimulate the economy by providing and array of economic benefits. 1) Numerous studies demonstrate that linear parks and greenways can increase nearby *property values*, this in turn increases local tax resources. 2) It can generate *spending by local residents* on greenway related activities $100 billion business. 3) Greenways often provide *new business opportunities* and locations for commercial activities. 4) Greenways are often major tourist attractions—(e.g., Blue Ridge Parkway generates $1.8 billion a year in tourist related expenditures). 5) Greenways figure in corporate relocation decisions

Greenways are really links in a chain of opportunities that can begin in your own backyard. These opportunities can begin by recognizing the potential of each and every piece of open land.

- urban
- rural
- suburban

Greenways allow us to treat land and water as a system. As interlocking pieces in a puzzle *not* as isolated entities.

You're fortunate and unique in already having a framework in place for a region-wide network of greenways. Much of this framework involves the Blue Ridge Parkway which could serve as the central artery for a system that extends into nearby communities and links the natural and cultural sites of the region.

Your efforts to preserve and promote the heritage of the Southern Appalachians is unalterably linked to your success in building on the success of the Blue Ridge Parkway, and using scenic byways as links between parks and nearby communities.

While there is a special magic and power to greenways that don't provide all the answers, North Carolina will need to continue its efforts to protect large natural areas. We need both hubs and links.

## CONCLUSION

I would like to conclude by complimenting the Appalachian Consortium, Friends of the Blue Ridge Parkway, and the National Park Service for their bold leadership in working to create a program that balances economic development and environmental protection to produce a sustainable future for the Southern Highlands.

I would also like to ask you to think briefly about the psychological and social value of greenways and open space. Why save ridgelines, forests, farmland, open spaces and other special places?

Why do people feel a sense of loss like losing a loved one or a friend when a historic building is demolished, a scenic view destroyed or a grove of trees bulldozed? It is not because we don't have lots of other trees in this country or lots of other buildings—it is because our sense of identity as *individuals*, as *Americans, and as citizens* of North Carolina are profoundly affected by special buildings, places and views.

John Costonis, dean of the Vanderbilt University School of Law, calls these special places the "icons of our environment". Icons, like the Grandfather Mountain, Roan Mountain, the Roanoke Farmers Market, or the historic buildings of Asheville, Black Mountain or Blowing Rock, are invested with *rich symbolic* significance that contributes to our identity and sense of belonging—no less than religion, language, or culture. This is an idea that goes back a very long way. For example, in ancient Rome there was a maxim that said, "A city should preserve the visible symbols of its identity to give citizens a sense of security in a changing world." More recently, Anthropologist Margaret Mead said, "The destruction of things that are familiar and important causes great anxiety in people."

Environmental quality aside, what we really trying to preserve I believe, is memory. It is an attempt to keep a mental grip on familiar and accustomed environments that make us feel comfortable and secure. The justification for creating greenways, preserving natural areas, historic buildings, special landscapes and scenic views has as much to do with our need for psychological stability and cultural continuity as they do with beauty and ecology. The mountains, forests, open spaces, and historic buildings of North Carolina are a resource both to the economy and to the psychology of this area.

The work of the Appalachian Consortium is fundamentally about connections. Connections between people and land; between conservation and economic development. About quality of life, about the future and about planning for it.

We can grow without destroying the things we love. The landscape and waterscapes of North Carolina are worth preserving not just because they are fragile, beautiful and resource-rich, but because they are emblematic of the South.

# The Urban Park of Oporto, Portugal
*Sidónio Costa Pardal*

During the preparation of the Master Plan for the City of Oporto in the 1960s, Urban Planner Robert Auzelle reserved an area of 100 hectares (approximately 247 acres) for a future urban park along Boavista Avenue near the sea. The site of the proposed park was approximately 5 kilometers from downtown and consisted of a patchwork quilt of individual landowners. A large portion of the site was abandoned farm land which had been neglected over the years and the site was being used for clandestine dumping of refuse. In the northeast corner of the site was the nucleus of a primitive farm which was still in operation utilizing farming methods which were centuries old.

The City of Oporto proceeded to purchase the land, parcel by parcel, and by 1982 when 60% of the site had been purchased, a decision was made to start the planning process for the park. Since the city government was not sure of what the park should consist and were besieged by a myriad of proposals for theme gardens, sports complexes, popular fairs, and industrial expositions, they solicited professional help from the Center for Urban Regional Studies (CESUR) at the Technical University of Lisbon.

Not only had Auzelle's vision become a reality, but the situation presented opportunities for study: the value of an urban park in today's society; methods of integration of an urban park into the matrix of the modern city; user needs which could be fulfilled by an urban park; and the justification of the use of strategic urban land and tax dollars for an urban park.

Human culture sometimes suffers from lapses of memory; ideas and knowledge fall by the wayside and are forgotten, only to resurface centuries later to inspire dazzling "renaissances" and furnish material for the most striking innovations of the avant garde. The design of urban parks has long been obscured by just such an eclipse of history. A grandiose period when cities built themselves cathedrals in the open air, "great machines for thinking" (in "Lotus Internacional," no. 30), such as the 19th century was, suddenly came to an end, succeeded only by the pale shadow of ornamental gardening. In urban design, parks came to be no more than green spaces, created without any clear understanding of their role or purpose. The aesthetic standards of landscape design declined significantly. In these circumstances the challenge of designing a park for the City of Oporto called for a return to the theories of the masters of the English School, to the sublime paradises of Prince Pückler, and the pastoral idylls of Olmsted.

While the experiments and styles of Italian and French gardens have had an undeniable influence on the conquest of large areas of external space as a complement or an adjunct to a house, it would be incorrect to conclude that the town park descends directly from them, as a variation on the traditional garden. Vaux-le-Vicomte, by Andre Le Nôtre, undoubtedly represents a new way of being in the world, a new way of constructing the world as a landscape of artifice. It is interesting to see how, in subsequent years, the influence of this garden, through the interpretations of William Kent, surface in the origins of the English Landscape School. One of Le Nôtre's merits lies in the way he goes beyond the traditional garden to reveal landscape on a large scale, freeing us from closed spaces and using a new language that expresses itself in wooded borders, clearings, large expanses of water, and long vistas that bring infinity right up to the house.

It is important to employ the knowledge acquired through historical research in examining the questions posed by urban development in our own time, when the concept of green spaces is a confused mixture of advertising slogans and vague expressions of some idealized compensation for our sense of discomfort and shortcomings of the urban environment. The labels "open space" and "green area" cast no light on the nature of the thing or the need to which it is a response. On the contrary, it is clear that this lack of definition has spawned a plague of empty spaces, miniature gardens and decorative embankments scattered without rhyme or reason across the urban landscapes of the last thirty years.

The grammar of external spaces was clear and coherent in the urban structure of the 19th century, little affected by speculation in an age when land was still valued according to the criteria of an agricultural society. Squares, parks, public gardens, and such, were the manifestations of a collective and civic notion of the city, understood as an organic whole in which the overriding consideration is the good of society and the well-being of the people, the city's inhabitants and users.

Although in the 19th century it was not unusual for a municipal council to have sufficient land at its disposal for building public parks and gardens, the same is not longer true. Contemporary urban management is caught between major contradictions on a battleground of multiple and complex conflicts of interest which constitute severe obstacles to enlightened planning. Hence, they face the problems of congestion, of shortages of space, or rushed expansion and change with little forethought and scant architectural consideration.

A new urban park is a rarity. We are out of the habit of designing such parks, and this presented us with a fresh problem. Contemporary writing on urban planning, architecture, and the plastic arts has virtually nothing to say about the experience of creating urban parks. The most interesting literature on the subject dates back to the 18th and 19th centuries. Curiously, and happily, many key writings were reissued in the 1970s and there was a revival of interest that acquired momentum throughout the 1980s with the exhibitions of Repton's designs and writings in London in February 1982, and the republication at the same time of *Red Books*, and later on, *Observations on the Theory and Practice of Landscape Gardening*.

It was not without misgivings that we approached the fact that the most up-to-date concepts of urban parks available to us had been developed in Birkenhead, Branitz, and New York more than a century ago. Naturally enough, we submitted the principles adopted in those far-off times to a close and methodical critique and assessed the success of those projects in terms of their capacity for survival and their practical utility in this day and age. In addition to this, we made an analysis of different user needs and the space requirement of specific uses for the City of Oporto.

In addressing the needs of users and capacities required, we made an exhaustive study to ascertain the amount of space required for each user need and to make sure that the use of these 100 hectares did not take away from the essential needs of the city for hospitals, schools, housing, and other vital uses. From the data gleaned from this part of the analysis, it was determined that the 500,000 population of Oporto required 250 hectares of urban open space. Since the existing open space in the form of gardens, small parks and other urban open spaces of the City of Oporto amount to about 100 hectares, the new park would bring the total to 200 hectares. The team recommended that the city set aside and reserve 50 additional hectares for future open space needs. The park as designed can accommodate up to 20,000 visitors at any peak period of time without any damage to the park.

After completion of the analysis, it was determined that the urban park could not be just a sports complex, a theme garden, or a collection of native oddities, but it had to be quantifiable open space, free of constraints which would generate and encourage spontaneous activities or provide the solace for passive and contemplative recreation. Furthermore, the concept of the park must be idealized nature which the urban dweller seeks, but seldom finds in today's urban jungle.

In order to make this concept a reality, we recommended that the park had to be safe from traffic and road noise; a combination of forested areas, rolling greensward and water areas; and formal plazas, meeting areas, and "fresh" houses (structures where one can escape from the rays of the hot summer sun; a feature of the Portuguese landscape for centuries).

The scale on which urban parks are laid out must be daring because their sheer size plays an essential role in successfully re-creating a sense of the beauty of nature within the bounds of a city and creating their own internal time. They must open up distances that afford an opportunity for the visitor to contemplate the world and meditate. In this sense, urban parks constitute a link between the city and the universe; they reinvest the daily life of the city's inhabitants with a sense of the true dimensions of the world. The concept of the urban park enables urban planners to deal with the city in a positive way.

As a park is built, it testifies to the possibility of constructing a landscape. Inherent in such an event there is a kind of nostalgia—a world of memories and a desire to give material shape that is unattainable. It is in this way that a park assumes a poetic dimension, a whiff of the sublime that is unmistakably romantic in inspiration.

Art cannot free itself of its symbolic nature. A park is dominated by what appears to be an aesthetic of nature, but this is only an appearance. For it is also—How could it be otherwise?—the urban antithesis of the urban.

# Managing Change: The Blue Ridge Parkway as a Museum of Managed American Countryside

*Nancy K. Robinson*

## Abstract

*The Blue Ridge Parkway was designed specifically by the concept of a "museum of the managed American countryside." Stanley Abbott designed the Parkway to offer visitors a glimpse of the then remote Appalachian subsistence agricultural practices: haystacks, horse-drawn plows, log cabins, outbuildings, vegetable gardens, etc. Over the years changes have come to the mountains that have altered farm scenes. Gone are the days when farmer and ox walk the plow, while women and children follow behind planting seed. Many who used to seek out a living through subsistence agriculture have kept their land but have taken jobs in related occupations in nearby towns and are weekend farmers only. Second homes and resort communities are encroaching on the Parkway's boundaries, changing viewsheds in agricultural areas. This paper will examine the original design, explore these changes, offer management options and present a concept for the design of an interpretive tool, an audio tape, as a means of perpetuating the museum concept today and in the future.*

In 1943, Stanley Abbott, the Resident Landscape Architect and Acting Superintendent of the Blue Ridge Parkway, wrote a memo to a Regional Director in the National Park Service. In it he addressed a number of design issues:

> As a reference to the theme of the Parkway and its interpretive statement in the Master Plan will make clear, it is no simple matter to define irrevocably what a national parkway should be. We have no precedent as far as I know in the world. This project is 500 miles or as far from Washington to Boston.... Through much of its length the parkway goes through a "managed" landscape and I think it has been pretty clear and relatively unquestioned within the Service that the problem was to marry ourself to that managed landscape.... To a very real extent the Parkway is inextricably bound up with the community. I think that this should be looked upon as an opportunity to accomplish by means of the parkway idea a new sort of conservation in which the national parkway becomes a museum of the managed American countryside. This conception is a departure from the basic idea that is behind the national park and even state parks. (Abbott 1943, pp. 7-9)

Over time, the National Park Service initiated a number of "museum" programs (USDI 1941). It restored pioneer structures such as Mabry Mill and the Brinegar Cabin. It encouraged the production of mountain crafts and traditional farm products by offering these for sale at exhibits and gift shops. It organized a land leasing program to encourage farmers to continue their hill culture. It promoted the use of scenic easements to preserve important viewsheds outside the Parkway's boundaries.

Planning for the Parkway began in December 1933. Since that date, many changes have come to the Appalachians.

---

Figures could not be published here; see *CELA 93: Public Lands/scapes*, Volume 5. Copyright 1994 by the Landscape Architecture Foundation / Council of Educators in Landscape Architecture, 4401 Connecticut Avenue NW, Suite 500, Washington, DC 20008. Reprinted with permission.

Among the most significant are changes in agricultural practices. Gone are the days when farmer and ox walk the plow, while women and children follow behind planting seed or collecting the crop. Many who once eked out a living through subsistence agriculture have kept their land but work today in nearby towns and are weekend farmers only. Improved highways have made the Appalachians more accessible; second homes and resort communities are encroaching on the Parkway's boundaries.

The "managed American countryside" is changing in ways that the originators of the Parkway could not possibly have foreseen when the Parkway was planned. These changes raise important questions regarding the management of the "museum" concept. For example, how did the idea evolve? How important was this concept to the overall design of the Parkway? How much of the original concept is still being preserved and how do we effectively measure this? Why have changes occurred? How do we interpret to visitors the changes that have taken place in the park? This paper will briefly address these questions and offer a design concept for an auto audio tape as one management solution.

## Background

*How did the idea evolve?* The United States was feeling the full impact of the Depression in 1933 when Congress passed the National Recovery Act, a public works project established to relieve unemployment (Jolley 1970, p. 20). The Blue Ridge Parkway, under this act, was an employment project to connect the Skyline Drive, a road that passed through the Shenandoah National Park in Virginia, to the Smoky Mountains National Park in Tennessee and North Carolina. Stanley Abbott, previously with the Westchester County Parkways, a system in New York then receiving international acclaim, was chosen to head up the project.

America's first national parks were established primarily to preserve large expanses of scenic wilderness. The vast majority of these lands were western parks. The Blue Ridge Parkway was one of the first eastern parks and Abbott quickly recognized that eastern parks raised different management issues than western parks. While western parks had been established to preserve majestic wilderness, eastern lands had been settled. Some areas had been cleared for agriculture. Others had been timbered.

When 26-year-old Abbott took charge of this project there were no guidelines on how to build a 500-mile long, 1,000-foot wide national parkway in the southern Appalachians. He had the rare opportunity to provide a new kind of national park. Abbott and his team solved one set of problems only to find that their solutions presented new challenges. How important was the museum concept to the overall design of the Parkway? While an integral part of the Parkway's design, the museum concept was only one piece in the puzzle. Other components included designing the route, the road, the wayside parks and the landscape.

*Designing the Route.* Since the new parkway was to be an extension of the Skyline Drive, Abbott first studied its design. He quickly recognized similarities to western national parks. The Skyline Drive had been built along the ridge; all structures in view of the road had been removed and visitors drove through miles of pristine forest.

Abbott chose not to apply the same design principles to the Parkway. Because much of the land had been settled and farmed for years in western North Carolina and Virginia, he thought that a Parkway that simply followed the ridge of the Appalachians for 500 miles would provide a tedious driving experience for visitors. He preferred to design a road that followed the ridge for awhile, then dropped down into farm valleys, back into the forest and up to the ridge again. He wanted to provide visitors with much variety so they could spend days and even weeks enjoying the Appalachians. "One panorama following right on another, thinking that as fortissimo, doesn't make the interesting piece of music that fortissimo mixed with a little pianissimo provides" (Evison 1958, p. 12).

After the route was determined the states could begin the complex process of land acquisition. Here there were endless problems to solve. Often farmers had no deeds to their land. Years before settlers had simply claimed land and passed it down from one generation to the next, making legal property lines difficult to determine.

*Designing the Road.* The road, itself, was both designed and constructed in 44 sections, ranging in length from 5 to 15 miles, and installed by different contractors. The landscape architects, working for the National Park Service, were the designers of the Parkway. They consulted with engineers from the Bureau of Public Roads on the maximum acceptable slope of the road, specifications for the curvilinear alignment and the style and materials to be used on the tunnels, bridges and retaining walls.

The utmost care and thought went into road design and construction. For example, because there was a dearth of skilled labor, masonry contracts were awarded to a number of stonemasons of Spanish, Italian and South American origin, who, when necessary, brought foreign workers to the U.S.

*Designing The Wayside Parks.* While Abbott and his associates were making early reconnaissance trips to determine the route, they spotted areas that were particularly scenic for one reason or another. In an interview with Blue Ridge Parkway Historian, Herb Evison, in 1958, Abbott recalled:

> As we traveled through the mountains on general reconnaissance, favorite places came into our thinking and we might say to ourselves or out loud, "We ought to control this" or "A gem." . . . Our theory was a major park every sixty miles, and in between two lesser day-use areas. (Evison 1958, p. 35)

Recreation parks, varying in size from several hundred to several thousand acres, became another design element. These wayside parks were intended to give tourists a chance to picnic, hike and camp along the way.

*Designing The Landscape.* There was certainly no precedent in the National Park Service for a roadside landscaping project of this scale. Abbott's landscape programs were possible because he could employ Civilian Conservation Corps (CCC) and Work Projects Administration (WPA) workers. During the Parkway's peak construction period there were over 1,200 men employed at any given time in landscape improvement projects (Abbuehl 1948, p. 26).

These men worked to heal construction scars, plant ferns on rock outcrops and raise canopies to improve views. They also dug up native rhododendrons and azaleas before construction began and replanted them after it was finished.

The charming farmsteads with their haystacks and horse drawn plows, pumpkins and split-rail fences are what particularly caught the imagination of the landscape architects. A glimpse of this idealized view of Appalachia is what Abbott wanted to offer Parkway visitors.

But this idyllic interpretation of Appalachia was only one side of the coin. Appalachia was quaint and charming with its log cabins and horse drawn plows, but it was also impoverished. With more and more families wanting land, tillable fields were at a premium. Corn was important to feed their livestock so they planted corn in the same field year after year. They didn't rotate crops and couldn't afford to fertilize or lime the soil. In an interview with Herb Evison, William Hooper, the Parkway's agronomist in the 1940s, commented:

> The yield of corn, for instance, in most of these mountain counties was twenty bushels to the acre. We like to think that if anybody is making less than 100 bushels to the acre, they can't afford to cultivate it. . . . When you get a yield of corn of 20 bushels to the acre and you need 100, you have to have 5 acres to get 100 bushels. The result was they were plowing everything up. (Evison 1971, p. 17)

How was the Service to manage a piece of government land that passed through a countryside which communicated poverty and neglect? After they healed the construction scars, the park land would be healthy and visitors would see a green ribbon, the right-of-way, passing through an otherwise poorly tended landscape. Abbott (1948) concluded that the only answer was to work with the Parkway's neighbors to improve the lands adjacent to the Parkway. He hired an agronomist to oversee two programs. The Soil and Moisture Conservation Program healed erosions scars and restored land to forest which should never have been cultivated because of poor soils or steep slopes.

The second program was the Leasing Program. After the Service healed the erosion problems, limed, fertilized, and improved the soil, the agronomist leased the improved land back to the mountain people who could use it if they agreed to follow Parkway guidelines. The Leasing Program was, in a sense, both a program of education and conservation. The success of the Leasing Program, in the early years can be attributed to the agronomist, Bill Hooper. He became familiar with each farmer's family and property and was as concerned about looking out for their welfare as he was in protecting and promoting National Park Service values. "At that period of time, 1945, we were almost as interested in land that was adjoining us as we were in ourselves" *(Personal communication 1991).*

While the agronomist was managing these programs, the landscape architects were planning exhibits for visitors. Today there are 16 pioneer culture exhibits with log cabins, spring houses and log barns. Because of Stanley Abbott's genuine concern for the well-being of the Parkway's neighbors, he also wanted to promote the mountain culture by selling crafts and farm products at exhibits.

Abbott and his colleagues initiated scenic easements as another land management program, a device used originally in the Westchester Parkway System (Firth 1993, p. 52). With scenic easements, the National Park Service could preserve views and protect certain aesthetic values beyond its borders by entering into a contract with adjacent landowners. For a fee less than it would cost to buy the land fee simple, Parkway neighbors would agree not to construct buildings, erect billboards or cut timber.

In 1948, Ed Abbuehl, one of the first landscape architects, summarized the development of the Parkway up to that time:

> The initial concept of the Blue Ridge Parkway as a scenic road to connect the Shenandoah and Great Smoky Mountains National Parks has been realized. In laying out the road the

National Park Service has included a thousand and one of the "best views." ... To those of us who have had the privilege of seeing the Parkway grow from an idea to a reality, there has also come a wider concept of its purpose and function. ... The Southern Highlands supported a living civilization isolated from the outside world and little affected by it. The Blue Ridge Parkway cuts a slice through this and opens it to public view. ... The Parkway which merely threads the mountains has through its landscape treatment almost seemed to include the whole countryside. It is natural and fitting for it to become a "Living Museum" for the Southern Highlands, and a start has been made in that direction.
(Abbuehl 1948)

## Research Methodology

How much of the original concept is still being preserved? How do we effectively measure this and why have changes come about? The author focused site research on one section of the Parkway, Section 2C, located in North Carolina a few miles south of the Virginia border. This section, about 10 miles long, has within it three elements of the early "museum" programs: the Brinegar Cabin, an exhibit of pioneer culture once prevalent in this region; Doughton Park, over seven miles of upland pastures and split-rail fences within a Wayside Park; and Meadow Fork Valley, a more than two mile stretch of valley farmsteads.

To keep track of the many landscape features and projects, the landscape architects worked with Parkway Land Use Maps (PLUMs), drawn at a scale of 1":100'. One PLUM represents about 1/2 mile of roadway. There are over 900 PLUMs that cover the entire length of the Parkway. PLUMs included planting plans, fence lines, the location of barns, erosion control projects, scenic easements, exhibits, etc.

Because the PLUMs represent original design intent, they served as a primary guide in site analysis. The author used PLUMs to assess general change by comparing the 1940s design to 1988 aerial photos. This helped locate station points from which historic photos had been taken, determine agricultural field patterns and scenic easements, understand landscape intentions around historic structures and to locate views which the original designers considered significant.

Site analysis involved several stages. In the summer of 1992 the author drove Section 2C, stopping every 300 to 400 feet to compare the 1940s PLUMs to today's landscape. Of particular interest were fence lines, vegetation growth, field patterns, designated views, the locations of scenic easements, the treatment of landscapes around the Brinegar Cabin and general farm scenes. The second step was to research historic photos in the Blue Ridge Parkway archives, then locate and photograph the same views in today's landscape. Next, the author interviewed "old-time" leaseholders focusing on how farming practices and life-styles have changed. Finally, the author interviewed past and present Blue Ridge Parkway personnel, including William Hooper, with the assistance of Professor Richard Westmacott.

## Findings

*Brinegar Cabin.* The site consists of the cabin, the granary and a spring house, as well as a rail fence which once enclosed a vegetable garden. In the early days of the Parkway, Bill Hooper grew a field of flax within the rail fence enclosure. The interpretive plan provided for weaving demonstrations and a concession where textile crafts, baskets and farm products like jams, honey and molasses were sold.

Today the concession is closed. A seasonal ranger does demonstrate the loom in the summer on weekend afternoons. The flax field is no longer displayed. The site evokes a desolate feeling. The buildings stand locked, empty and quiet on the hillside and don't suggest the way they were when the Brinegars lived here with chickens clucking, kids playing in the yard and hogs burrowing for chestnuts in the nearby woods. The changes have come about primarily because of budget constraints. Barry Buxton, in his *Brinegar Cabin Historic Resource Study*, writes:

> The grounds of the site are currently kept meticulously mowed. This is not an accurate portrayal of the dusty, work-worn state of the grounds as once existed when the Brinegars were homesteading.... The grounds as they are currently maintained resemble a golf course or a city park, and are not at all historically accurate. (Buxton 1988, pp. 11-12)

*Doughton Park.* One's first impression driving through Doughton Park is that the original intent to preserve the wide, open, upland pastures has been successful. One is struck by the scenic, rail fences that stretch for miles along the roadside, enclosing rolling pastures. Upon closer examination of aerial photos and PLUMs, however, it becomes apparent that vegetation in many roadside areas have grown considerably.

Settlers traditionally built their rail fences of chestnut which is extremely durable. After the chestnut blight of the late 1920s and early 1930s Abbott had CCC and WPA workers cut and stockpile the wood. Hooper organized the erection of these fences. The stockpiles are running low and rails are now replaced with nontraditional locust. The difficulty in replacing rails may explain why certain worm fences that were originally indicated on the PLUMs are now straight-rail or post-and-wire. Second-home development threatens views in Doughton Park, as it does in other areas along the Parkway. Lands once intended as open pasture have been taken out of the agricultural lease program and allowed to revert to forest in order to screen new, second homes.

*Meadow Fork Valley.* Leaving Doughton Park, motorists descend gradually into Meadow Fork Valley where a stream flows. It has a number of small farmsteads throughout with views of pastures, barns and cattle grazing.

In the 1930s and 1940s the valley was dotted with tapered haystacks. Farmers had draft horses or oxen pulling plows. There were apple orchards and cherry trees in blossom in the spring. It was a charming valley of Appalachian farmsteads typical of what Abbott wanted to share with visitors. While there was no official interpretive plan for the valley, the farm scenes spoke for themselves.

Today, because of changing farm economics, the horse drawn plow has been replaced by the tractor; tapered haystacks have been replaced by round hay bales; and the apple orchards have died of old age and haven't been replaced. The majority of the leaseholders are in their 60s and 70s. They have a deep love for and commitment to their land and to the old ways of farm life. But, times are changing. Their children won't be continuing traditions here that have been carried on for generations.

## Discussion

*How much of the design is still viable?* To determine this the author categorized changes along Section 2C into three categories: natural, cultural and administrative.

*Natural Change.* Because the designers left very specific design instructions in the form of the PLUMs, the author briefly considered the feasibility of freezing the Parkway design in time and restoring the entire 500 miles to the design shown on the PLUMs. But one is quickly reminded that landscapes are living entities constantly undergoing change. Blights can kill an entire tree species, affecting not only the landscape but fence design as well. Storms like Hurricane Hugo can destroy woodlands, creating views which were not intended. Plants die of old age, removing entire orchards from the landscape.

*Cultural Change.* The Southern Highlands are becoming increasingly popular for recreation and retirement. Second home development is a manifestation of this trend. Today there are 23 million visitors to the Parkway, far exceeding estimates of the 1930s and 1940s. Increased visitation affects the management of exhibits.

Agricultural management of the Parkway is evolving due to changing farm economics, changing life-styles and aging leaseholders, resulting in visual changes in the landscape. Instead of haystacks of the 1940s we see round bales of the 1990s; hay sheds replace barns; tractors replace horses and plows.

*Administrative Change.* The early designers and agronomists have retired or are no longer living. Superintendents, rangers and maintenance crews have come and gone. And each time there's a changing of the guard, dilution inevitably takes place. Soon there won't be anyone left who remembers what was originally intended or how the landscape once looked. If change is inevitable and it is impossible to return the Parkway to the literal, historic design expressed on the PLUMs, what steps are necessary to retain historic integrity and provide for a "museum of the managed American countryside?"

## Administrative Recommendations

*Landscape research.* Performing thoughtful landscape research is the first requirement. Study the original plans, in this case the PLUMs. Research historic documents —photos, oral histories, master plans, letters, memos, early Agronomist Reports and early Soil and Moisture Conservation Reports.

*Update the PLUMs.* Working from copies of the original PLUMs (preserving the originals), new notations should be added to reflect current conditions. Abbott required rangers as well as maintenance staff to carry PLUMs in their vehicles and refer to them on a "daily" basis. Today, this practice is adhered to by some, but not all employees. It is a practice that should be reintroduced and reinforced.

*Reinstate an agronomist.* After Bill Hooper retired in the mid- 1960s, he was not replaced. Over time he had become teacher, protector and friend to the Parkway's neighbors. He was key to the success of the Leasing Program. Today's rangers, who have numerous responsibilities, also manage the leasing program. There are over 400 leasing permits issued through the agricultural land use program with agricultural lands encompassing over 150 miles of right-of-way. A full-time agronomist is needed to help farmers address the complexities of their changing economy.

*Establish land trusts.* Many longtime property owners whose lands adjoin the Parkway have expressed a true love for the land and a concern for its future. Land trusts would allow them to sell their land at current real estate prices, or deed it to children and grandchildren and, at the same time, protect development rights. Many rural landowners fear that the government will buy up more and more land. A private, regional, land trust organized to serve the 4,000 adjacent landowners might alleviate that fear, offer an alternative to large scale development, and keep the land in the private sector.

## Interpretative Recommendations

*One question remains.* Old time Appalachia is no more. The charming elements of the pioneer culture that Abbott hoped to provide to visitors are missing from the landscape. How do we interpret the museum concept to visitors?

It isn't reasonable in today's economy to ask farmers to continue uneconomical farming practices and financing more than 150 miles of living history farms is cost-prohibitive for the Parkway. One possible solution is to add a new component to the existing interpretive program by providing an auto, audio tape.

*Questions immediately arise.* For example, should a single tape relate the entire story—the history, design and management problems? Or should a variety of tapes be produced to address themes, such as "The Museum of the Managed American Countryside" or "The Blue Ridge Parkway as a Designed Landscape"? Should a tape spell out in detail the stories? Or should it tell just enough to provoke thought and raise questions? Should a single tape cover the entire length of the Parkway from beginning to end? Should there be a tape for North Carolina and another for Virginia? Should there be one tape for motorists traveling north, and another for those going south? How often do the tapes have to be updated? Are there resources available to provide material for audio tapes?

To begin to answer these questions, the author reviewed the current interpretive program for the Parkway and turned to some of its known authorities, such as Freeman Tilden and Joseph Shomon, for guidance. Briefly, the current interpretive program includes 16 pioneer exhibits, the sale of handicrafts and farm products at gift shops and visitor centers (not exhibits), and 55 displays at exhibits and overlooks that comment on places of historical and natural interest. In addition, William Lord, one of the first directors of the Interpretive Division, has written a two volume paperback *Blue Ridge Parkway Guide* (1990). The guide lists, by milepost, sites of interest, gives a succinct history of the region, describes the significance of most of the 264 overlooks and illustrates the flora and fauna in the area. The Blue Ridge Parkway also publishes the *Parkway Milepost,* a promotional newsletter targeted to visitors.

An excellent opportunity is being missed in the current interpretive program. The story behind the design and construction of the Parkway is as significant a story in American history as the building of the Erie Canal or the Brooklyn Bridge; yet nowhere along the route is this aspect of the Parkway story being told in a systematic manner. One gets bits and pieces along the route, such as the display at the Linn Cove viaduct visitor center which describes the engineering of the viaduct. There is a need to provide visitors with some insights into how the Parkway came to be and what was involved in that process.

In examining guidelines for interpretation, the author turned to Freeman Tilden and Joseph Shomon, among others. Briefly, according to Tilden, as described in his book, *Interpreting Our Heritage* (1977), good interpretation is provocative and stimulates the imagination of visitors, rather than simply telling a straightforward, factual story. Also, it is the interpreter's responsibility to provide visitors with a sense of the bigger picture, a sense of the whole, rather than simply feeding them facts and dates (Tilden 1977, p. 9). Shomon (1968, p. 23) adds, in his *Manual For Outdoor Interpretation,* that a successful interpretive plan for a national park should follow the tenets of the Master Plan for that park.

The following briefly summarizes answers to the questions posed above.

*One.* Should a single tape relate the entire story, or should a variety of tapes be produced to address themes? According to Abbott, "The Parkway was laid out with the expectation that many visitors would spend days or weeks along its route (Abbott 1948). Firth (1985, p. 74), in a report to the National Park Service on biotic cultural resources also states:

> The enjoyment of historic landscapes requires time. It is not a scene to be fixed and framed; to be briefly surveyed and instantly comprehended. Like a natural area, a historic district should invite longer stays for exploration and discovery—to appreciate a place in time.

The author, then, supports the idea of creating theme tapes which would invite visitors to return to the Parkway and each time discover different aspects of the story behind this remarkable national park.

*Two.* Should a tape be "didactic" and explicative or "provocative," raising questions for visitors to ponder? The Parkway design is conducive to both types of tapes. The "didactic" tape, the straightforward, typical format where a narrator tells a story in a linear fashion with a beginning, middle and end is well suited for places where people stop and spend more leisurely time—at visitor centers. The "didactic" format is difficult to apply, however, to a tape that one hears while driving through the landscape. In many instances, the narrator would not have time to tell a story about a landscape as one is passing through it. The scene passes too quickly. The experience of driving through a landscape and hearing about it would be difficult to synchronize.

A "provocative" approach is more appropriate for the automobile. To best understand the difference between the "didactic" and "provocative" approaches one can make an analogy to techniques in film direction, comparing early film direction to today's techniques. Many early films opened with a scroll rolling that set the scene. Viewers read, "Once upon a time . . ." and were introduced to the film in a rather simple, straightforward linear manner, representing the "didactic" approach. The scene was clearly set and little was left to the imagination.

Today's films, on the other hand, represent more closely a "provocative" design format. Most films today drop the viewer into a scene, with no explanation of the characters or the setting. Over a two-hour period, through such devices as flashbacks, dreams, and fantasies, the viewer develops an understanding for the characters. The process is gradual. It is accomplished by layering bits of information. Sometimes images flash onto the screen for only seconds, but an impression is created. By the end of the film, by experiencing one image laid on top of the next, viewers develop an understanding of the characters and a sense of "place," of time, of history, often without the facts ever having been explicitly spelled out.

The author proposes the use of similar devices in designing thematic auto, audio tapes for the Parkway. These tapes would provide a kind of auditory choreography of sounds and voices, music and pauses, all coordinated to the rhythm and design of the Parkway itself.

*Three.* Should a single tape cover the entire Parkway from beginning to end? Or, should there be a Virginia tape and 2 North Carolina tape? If one is designing by themes, the "museum" tape should relate primarily to landscapes between Blowing Rock in North Carolina, milepost 280, and Roanoke, Virginia, milepost 120. This is the stretch where most of the agricultural leases are located. To develop tapes by state would provide a bifurcated vision of the Parkway. In other words, the tapes should be created to fit themes, rather than artificial geographic parameters.

*Four.* Should designers create one tape for motorists traveling north and another for those going south? The script should address the specific landscapes one passes, and views would, of course, vary, depending on the direction one travels. Also, there are numerous stories to tell and visitors could enjoy a completely different set of anecdotes when traveling north than south.

*Five.* How often would the tapes have to be updated? Because the "museum" tape would address Parkway history (which won't change), as well as cultural trends which will continue to evolve (but probably won't change radically for some time), revisions can be kept to a minimum on both types of tapes.

*Six.* Are there resources available to produce interpretive audio tapes? In 1978 the National Park Service cosponsored the Blue Ridge Parkway Folklife Project. This was a field survey of the region, conducted by the American Folklife Center of the Library of Congress, which recorded many aspects of Appalachian cultural traditions. The project undoubtedly offers a wealth of information.

Herb Evison, an historian for the Parkway, interviewed Stanley Abbott, Bill Hooper, Ed Abbuehl and others. Tapes and transcripts are filed in the National Park Service facility in Harper's Ferry, Virginia. Because the tapes are old, the quality may or may not be adequate for reproduction. If not, actors could listen to them for voice tones, inflections, and the energy and attitudes of Abbott and others and try to approximate the original speakers.

## Sample tape design for section 2C

The author developed the concept for a sample tape, focusing on the three landscapes within Section 2C discussed previously: the Brinegar Cabin, Doughton Park and Meadow Fork Valley. The following briefly discusses the process:

First, the author analyzed interviews with the early designers, Bill Hooper and early leaseholders. Comments seemed to fall into three categories: Historic Features; Blue Ridge Parkway Museum Programs; and Current Threats to Museum Programs. These three categories provided focus for the script of the tape.

The author decided to record only sounds or voices heard in the early days of the Parkway, "museum" sounds. Because Bill Hooper was such a key figure in the success of the "museum" concept, his voice is used for narration. Each time his voice is heard, a new aspect of the Parkway story is about to be introduced.

Several design criteria were taken into account. Although the design speed of the Parkway is 45 miles per hour, the author designed the tape for a driving speed of 35 miles per hour to give more time to relay a story. To provide variety, the author consciously juxtaposed male voices and female voices, older voices with younger voices and voices with varying inflections and accents.

The rhythm of the tape also fits the rhythm of the passing landscape. For instance, in Meadow Fork Valley where numerous issues are represented in a short distance, the author recorded five brief anecdotes, each less than a minute in length. But as motorists travel north, leaving the valley, they enter Doughton Park and drive 6.2 miles past pastures and miles of rail fences until reaching the Brinegar Cabin. This stretch provides an opportunity for more in-depth comments. For Doughton Park, the author assembled lengthier anecdotes. Bill Hooper describes early burning practices, erosion problems and how the leasing program helped farmers restore their land. At milepost 238.5 the motorist enters the parking lot at the Brinegar Cabin. This stopping place offers the opportunity for lengthier stories about the Brinegars and about the concession that once operated from the Cabin.

All quotes are site specific, intentionally chosen to give motorists a "sense of place." In the Meadow Fork Valley segment, for example, the voices heard are those of residents whose families have been living in the valley since the Parkway was built.

Any one landscape represents a myriad of past and present issues. Obviously, all issues cannot be addressed in the brief time it takes to pass by that landscape. Again, taking Meadow Fork Valley as an example, it is important to keep in mind that there are other valleys prior to and following this section which portray many of the same issues characteristic of Meadow Fork Valley. Ideas not mentioned in this portion of the tape could be covered when traveling through other farmstead valleys.

## Conclusion

A limitation of a project of this scale is its labor intensity and requisite research team. In addition, particularly because of the time it would take to review the Folklife material, interview leaseholders, edit segments so as to match the Parkway design, etc. the project could be costly. One would have to coordinate a variety of foundation grants or find investors. There is certainly a potential market, with 23 million visitors a year. And, because the tapes require very few revisions, once produced, this method would be far more cost effective in the long run than trying to manage living history farms for more than 150 miles. Distribution and marketing techniques need to be explored further.

Finally, both Bill Hooper and Ed Abbuehl are in their 80s, as are many of the other early contributors such as stone masons, CCC workers and leaseholders. There is some urgency to record peoples' memories while they are still able, healthy and vibrant.

## REFERENCES

Abbott, Stanley W. 1943. "Confidential memo for regional director Taylor, Region One." Asheville, NC: USDI National Park Service. Blue Ridge Parkway Archives, Series 38, Box 48, Folder 5.

Abbott, Stanley W. 1948. "Parkways--Past, Present and Future." *Parks & Recreation*. 31(12): 681-691.

Abbuehl, Edward. 1948. "History of the Blue Ridge Parkway." In *For a Ranger Conference*. Asheville, NC: USDI National Park Service. Blue Ridge Parkway Archives, RG 51, Series 41, Box 51, Folder 7.

Buxton, Barry M. 1988. *Brinegar Cabin Historic Resource Study*. Asheville, NC: USDI. National Park Service. Blue Ridge Parkway.

Evison, S. Herbert. 1958. Interview of Stanley Abbott, Blue Ridge Parkway landscape architect. Transcript held at USDI National Park Service office, Harper's Ferry, VA.

Evison, S. Herbert. 1971. Interview of William O. Hooper, Blue Ridge Parkway agronomist. Transcript held at USDI National Park Service office, Harper's Ferry, VA.

Firth, Ian J. W. 1985. "Biotic Cultural Resources: Management: Considerations for Historic Districts in the National Park System, Southeast Region." *Research Management Report* SER-82. Atlanta: USDI National Park Service. Southeast Regional Office.

_____. 1993. *Blue Ridge Parkway Historic Resource Study*. Athens, GA: University of Georgia. For USDI, National Park Service, Southeast Region.

Jolley, Harley E. 1970. *The Blue Ridge Parkway*. Knoxville, TN: University of Tennessee Press.

Lord, William G. 1990. *Blue Ridge Parkway Guide*. (2 vols.) New York: Eastern Acorn.

Shomon, Joseph P. (ed.) 1968. *Manual of Outdoor Interpretation*. New York: National Audobon Society.

Tilden, Freeman. 1977. *Interpreting Our Heritage*. Chapel Hill: University of North Carolina Press.

USDI. 1941. *Master Development Plan: Blue Ridge Parkway: Second Edition*. National Park Service. Branch of Plans and Designs.

# Beauty and Utility: Preserving the Urban Parkway
*Peter S. Szabo*

How do you preserve the character of a unique and historic parkway while attempting to meet the needs of the 60,000 drivers who use it each day? Since early 1992, the Connecticut Department of Transportation (DOT) has been working to address this question. The end result of this process will be guidelines for DOT treatment of Connecticut's Merritt Parkway and the implementation of a plan of action for scenic and aesthetic improvement. This presentation will provide an overview of the process used to arrive at these ends.

## The Merritt Parkway—History

Constructed in the 1930s by the Connecticut Highway Department, the full length of the Merritt Parkway opened to traffic in 1940. The parkway was built over and around rolling hills of forests and farmland in Fairfield County Connecticut, with two lanes in each direction covering 37.5 miles from the New York state line to the Housatonic River. The road sits on the north half of a 300-foot right-of-way. The parkway's original planners had expected that the south half of the right-of-way would some day be used for expanding the roadway, though the 150-foot wide, 37.5-mile long forested ribbon has, over the years, become an integral part of the parkway's rustic character. The Merritt Parkway was the first grade-separated, limited-access roadway in Connecticut. More than 70 bridges carry the parkway over local roads, or allow for passage over the parkway. These bridges were designed by Connecticut Highway Department architect George Dunkelberger. Dunkelberger gave each bridge a unique design, employing art deco and art moderne styles. The parkway's original designed landscape was stunning. Landscape architect Thayer Chase applied a naturalistic philosophy, using native plant materials to gently blend the scars of construction into adjacent woods and meadows.

The Merritt Parkway was planned so that Fairfield County Connecticut (essentially, a distant suburb of New York City) could be opened to broader settlement and development. To this end, the parkway has succeeded, though development has also increased pressures on the roadway. Drawing distinct pleasure from its unique character, residents in the area feel a tremendous sense of ownership towards the parkway.

## The Merritt Parkway and the Blue Ridge Parkway

The Merritt Parkway and the Blue Ridge Parkway are similar in the name "parkway." However, while the immediate environment of the Merritt Parkway is still largely forested and scenic, its use and general surrounding development pattern classifies it as an urban parkway. The contrast between the Merritt and the Blue Ridge is highlighted by the following statistic: While 8.6 million vehicles travelled the 469 miles of the Blue Ridge Parkway in 1992 (National Park Service figures), the 37.5 miles of the Merritt Parkway carried 18.6 million vehicles. In other words, though it is less than one-tenth the length of the Blue Ridge, the Merritt Parkway carries twice the traffic volume.

This makes the challenge of preserving the Merritt Parkway highly complex.

## The Merritt Today

The Merritt today carries nearly 60,000 vehicles each day. Travelling speeds often exceed 60-65 miles per hour. Fairfield

County has become one of the richest counties in America; many of its residents live there both for its countrified setting and its proximity to New York City. Many commuters on the Merritt are headed to work in Westchester County (in neighboring New York state), New York City, or at businesses in the area. Since the mid-1970s, numerous American corporations have moved their corporate headquarters to office parks set in rustic, forested, quiet locations along the Merritt Parkway in lower Fairfield County.

## BACKGROUND OF THE PRESERVATION EFFORT

Two factors set the stage for renewed conflict over the future of the Merritt Parkway in early 1991.

First, the Connecticut Department of Transportation was conducting a study of transportation needs in southwestern Connecticut. One option, among many considered, was to double the size of the Merritt Parkway, using the other half the state-owned right-of-way as the parkway's builders had intended.

Second, the Connecticut Trust for Historic Preservation was leading an effort to have the Merritt Parkway listed on the National Register of Historic Places. The Merritt was so-listed in early 1991.

And yet, two factors were also setting the stage for the preservation effort to come.

First, Connecticut voters elected Lowell P. Weicker, Jr. as their Governor in 1990. Early on in his administration, Governor Weicker stated his commitment to preserving the unique character of the Merritt Parkway, suggesting the widening option would not be pursued.

Second, Governor Weicker appointed Emil H. Frankel as Commissioner of the Connecticut Department of Transportation. Though the initial experience with preservation advocates was rocky, Commissioner Frankel was, and has remained, committed to preserving Merritt's unique character. Late in 1991, the Commissioner initiated a strategic review to examine all proposed major State transportation projects as well as the Department's expected financial resources for the next ten years. This strategic review resulted ultimately in a halting of design of several major projects, and included a significant refocus of the southwest corridor study. This study no longer includes the Merritt-widening option. A reading of the strategic review also suggests that the finances which would be required for Merritt expansion will not be available for many years.

In the summer of 1991, the Commissioner initiated early discussions on formation of a group to advise him on Merritt Parkway issues.

A conference in Southport, Connecticut in the fall of 1991 highlighted preservationist concerns about the Merritt. At this conference, DOT Deputy Commissioner Michael Saunders reaffirmed the Governor's and the Commissioner's position that no widening of the Merritt Parkway would be pursued in Weicker administration.

### The Merritt Parkway Working Group

In the summer of 1991, Commissioner Frankel decided to form a working group of Department officials and outside individuals to advise him on ways to preserve the unique character of the Merritt Parkway, while also maintaining what is an important transportation artery as a safe and efficient roadway.

Three outside advisors from the fields of preservation, landscape architecture, and architecture met with the Commissioner in January 1992 and agreed to join the effort. A fourth outside advisor, from the historic preservation field, joined in the fall of 1992.

Representatives on the working group from the DOT now include the Deputy Commissioner of Engineering and Highway Operations, his Executive Assistant, the head of Highway Maintenance for District III (which includes the Merritt), the Manager of State Design, the Manager of Traffic Engineering, the Assistant District Engineer of Construction for District III, the head of Landscape Design, the Director of Property and Facilities Services (which manages the six Mobil Marts on the parkway), and the Assistant Director for Intermodal Planning. In addition, the Connecticut Division Administrator from the Federal Highway Administration became a member of the group earlier in 1993.

The Merritt Parkway Working Group (MPWG) met for first time in March of 1992, and has met approximately monthly since then. Almost every meeting has been chaired by the Commissioner.

In the spring of 1992 the DOT engaged a National Park Service team to conduct a Historic American Building Survey/Historic American Engineering Record (HABS/HAER) documentation of the Merritt Parkway during the summer of 1992.

The HABS/HAER project helped to set a baseline of information for the working group and to begin to focus the DOT's attention on the parkway.

During this process Commissioner Frankel decided not to stop Merritt projects underway or about to be bid. The state was in the deepest economic decline in more than 50 years, and pressure to get construction work out on the streets was great.

Over the course of the first six months, the group discussed major problems facing the parkway. Eventually six major issue areas were outlined: landscape, design, bridges, facilities, traffic control devices/signs, and maintenance. In the summer of 1992, the group decided to prepare guidelines and a list of improvement actions for each of these areas to be recommended to Commissioner Frankel.

Some examples of challenging problems and the proposals for how to address them include:

### Design standards

- Challenge: How to address the pressure of American Association of State Highway and Transportation design standards for expressways on the character of the roadway. (For example, pressures to straighten and widen the roadway, to clear vegetation, use guiderails extensively, etc.)

- Response: The group's approach has been to set standards for the aesthetic realm (parkway standards) wherever it can, infuse AASHTO standards with aesthetics where possible, and apply AASHTO alone where it must. The working group pursued this philosophy in drawing up the guidelines.

### Landscape

- Challenge: The landscape was identified by the MPWG as one of two central elements of the parkway's unique character. The original plantings are now 50 years old. Resources for maintenance and replacement are scarce. There is a good deal of overgrowth.

- Response: The group communicated to the Department the importance of giving the Parkway special care (the response: an effort to clear underbrush and overgrowth away from bridge abutments). The MPWG set guidelines for DOT actions in this area. In addition, a consultant was engaged this summer to create a Landscape Master Plan for entire Parkway --funded by ISTEA Enhancement money. The master plan will include guidance and schematic concepts, so that planting plans may be easily produced from it.

## Bridges

- Challenge: The bridges were identified by the MPWG as the other central element of the Parkway's unique character. Many are more that 50 years old. The MPWG emphasized that preserving architectural detail, and restoring and replicating structures needs to be done sensitively.

- Response: The group set guidelines for this area. In addition, the Department is in the process of engaging a consultant (with expertise in working with aged concrete structures) to prepare a preservation plan for the bridges. This plan will focus on detail —including specifications for concrete restoration and care. The group also considered the idea of lighting the architectural details on the exterior of the bridges in a monument-like style.

## The Median

- Challenge: Median plantings are now 50 years old. Many died in the severe environment (salt from winter plowing operations). Guiderails were added to prevent cross-over accidents. Some jersey barrier is used under bridges. Parkway supporters are vehemently opposed to the cutting of trees. The working group wrestled with the issue of how to restore a comprehensive aesthetic concept to the median that is consistent with the Merritt's character.

- Response: Guidelines have been proposed for the median. The Landscape Master Plan will also present some ideas about median treatments. In addition, a study of alternative guiderail systems for use along scenic and historic roadways is underway.

## The Roadside Area

- Challenge: The roadside area once blended the roadway into the forest and the countryside in a naturalistic fashion. Now the plantings are 50 years old. Thousands of mountain laurel (Connecticut's state flower) are overly shaded and sprawling, most are obscured from view or dead. Guiderail has been added to protect motorists from hitting mature trees near the roadway. Major guide and other signs are a mish mash of styles. The working group considered how to restore the naturalistic feel while still meeting safety requirements. Another major question was the treatment of the remaining right of way: How to manage a 150 foot wide, 37.5 mile long forest?

- Response: Guidelines have been proposed in this area. The Landscape Master Plan and the guiderails study will provide additional ideas. Many signs have already been removed. A consultant was engaged to develop a distinct signing scheme.

Overall, an important challenge is how to get sufficient resources to the Merritt Parkway. Commissioner Frankel has suggested that a Merritt Parkway Conservancy be established to bring level of care to the parkway over and above what the DOT can provide.

This past May, Governor Weicker designated the Merritt Parkway as a state Scenic Road at a ceremony at the Greenwich service area.

Through further dialogue and some

meetings with citizens and outside groups, the draft guidelines were completed in July 1993.

The next step is public comment. Two public meetings are scheduled for October in two locations in Fairfield County.

## THE FUTURE

What does the future hold, both for the guidelines process and for the parkway itself?

Many issues remain to be addressed. One is the advisory structure for ongoing public involvement in Merritt-related challenges. The Merritt Parkway Working Group was always intended to be a transient institution. Once guidelines are formally adopted by the Department, it is expected that the group's work will have come to an end and it will be dissolved. Since the mid-1970s there has existed a Merritt Parkway Advisory Committee, which has been loosely and infrequently consulted by the DOT on Merritt matters. Proposals to broaden the range of participation on that committee to include official representation from professional groups concerned with the Merritt and to regularize the meetings between the group and DOT officials are currently being considered.

Another central issue is the funding mechanism for Merritt Parkway aesthetic improvements. What is the proper level of public resources that should be brought to bear on the parkway? Is there a new role for private resources? The Commissioner has suggested that a Merritt Parkway Conservancy be created as a private, nonprofit organization to channel private funds into landscaping, restoration, and other projects and efforts related to the Merritt Parkway. This idea is beginning to be explored.

Once finalized, the guidelines will become DOT policy on the treatment of the Merritt. They will be consulted by designers, construction inspectors, and maintenance and other DOT professionals when carrying out projects on the parkway. In addition, as the parkway has been listed on the National Register of Historic Places, the guidelines will form the basis for a Memorandum of Understanding with the State Historic Preservation Office for treatment of the Merritt.

A landscape master plan for the parkway is currently under way. Once this plan has been completed, it is expected that a series of landscape restoration projects consistent with the schematics and philosophy outlined in the master plan will be carried out by the Department.

In addition, the Department is in the process of contracting for bridge conservation consulting services. The bridge conservation consultant will develop a plan for bridge restoration and preservation, which will include specifications on the rehabilitation of historic concrete, best practices to follow when duplicating architectural detail, and current state of the art in other restoration practices.

The DOT is also conducting an evaluation of aesthetic guiderail treatments to be used on scenic and historic roads, and, possibly, the Merritt Parkway.

## LESSONS

There have been many lessons learned from the Merritt Parkway Working Group process.

First, any preservation effort of this sort needs demonstrated, firm commitment from the top in order to succeed. For example, in this process, the Governor stated his commitment to maintaining the unique character of the Merritt. In addition, Commissioner Frankel chaired almost every meeting over the course of a year and a half. These signals are vital to communicating the priority of the effort to the engineers, maintainers, and other transportation professionals who are the day-to-day stewards of the character of the resource.

A second lesson is to use outside expertise where possible and prudent. Outside experts freshen and elevate the level of discussion. They bring valuable knowledge, judgement, and creativity to preservation issues. They help to build credibility with vital constituencies and with the public. So long as the outside experts selected to join in this kind of an effort are patient and open minded, there is a high probability that successful levels of trust and communication can be built.

A third lesson is that, ultimately, financial resources are a vital element of any preservation initiative. One may devise the highest quality plans possible, but financial resources are required to put them into action. While the ISTEA Enhancement Program is a valuable source of funding, private financing will inevitably be necessary to supplement the level of care a DOT can give an historic resource.

Another important lesson: the Merritt Parkway Working Group increasingly realized that the Merritt's future is inextricably linked with surrounding land uses.

Malls, office parks, and housing developments all generate automobile traffic. In so much as these activities take place in the vicinity of the parkway, pressures to widen, straighten, and improve the safety of the roadway will increase. The group concluded that the land use decisions of the eight towns through which the Merritt passes will affect it's character as much as the decisions of the DOT.

The nature of the urban parkway brings with it particular preservation challenges. However, perhaps the most important lesson of the Merritt Parkway Working Group process has been that aesthetic requirements can be met while still meeting safety concerns, even though the resource is an extremely high-use facility, and there is pressure from engineering design standards.

---

If there are any questions about this process, please feel free to contact Peter S. Szabo, Executive Assistant, Office of the Commissioner, Connecticut Department of Transportation, at (203) 594-3003; or Ms. Maribeth Demma, Assistant Director of Intermodal Planning, at (203) 594-2134.

# Crisis in Viewshed Protection: Enlisting Community Support

*Jim Fox*

Land development near park boundaries looms as one of the National Park Service's major problems as we approach the 21st Century. Adjacent properties are highly desirable for residences and vacation homes because of spectacular settings and because of the protection afforded by neighboring federal ownership.

Adjacent lands are attractive to developers and entrepreneurs due to the recognized draw of millions of visitors to National Park Service areas, combined with frequently low land prices and lack of adequate land use controls in remote areas.

The park visitor's experience is seriously altered by nonconforming adjacent developments, and the National Park Service is impaired in its ability to protect and preserve park values.

There is a growing sense of awareness of external threats within the National Park Service. The report of the 75th Anniversary Symposium entitled "Our National Parks: Challenges and Strategies for the 21st Century," which was held in Vail, Colorado in October, 1991, set forth as part of "Strategic Objective No. 1 . . . Prevention of external and transboundary impairment of park resources and their attendant values should be a central objective of park system policy."

National parks do not exist in a vacuum, but are an integrated part of the larger community. We must be aware of the legitimate concerns of park neighbors, who welcome economic development in areas often suffering from a decline in agriculture and other traditional means of livelihood, yet hold true to our mandate to protect and preserve.

The Blue Ridge Parkway is one of the most spectacular, diverse and complex units of the National Park System. The Parkway may be thought of as a 470-mile long by several hundred-foot wide ribbon of a National Park stretching across the top of the Southern Appalachian Mountains connecting Shenandoah National Park to the north with Great Smoky Mountains National Park to the south. The Parkway winds through 29 counties, 6 Congressional districts, four national forests and one Indian reservation.

Nineteenth-century Scottish poet Thomas Campbell wrote, "'tis distance lends enchantment to the view and robes the mountain in its azure hue." Present-day park managers may take a more prosaic view of visual resources, but Campbell's description is basic to the concept of design and management of the Parkway.

The Parkway was carefully located, engineered and landscaped to afford the motorist prime examples of mountain culture, natural scenes and outstanding views sweeping from horizon to horizon and covering thousands of square miles. This sense of vastness is one of the Parkway's prime attractions. Annual visitation in excess of 20 million is striking testimony to the success of the Parkway concept and to the vision of the Parkway's founders.

Despite its great length, the Parkway's land base is relatively small, with approximately 80 thousand acres in federal ownership. Therefore, most distant views and many mid-range views are not of national park land.

The Act of Congress creating the National Park Service in 1916 directed the agency to conserve the scenery and other resources unimpaired for future generations. However, because so much of the Parkway's visual resource lies beyond its boundaries and outside of National Park Service control, the Parkway is particularly vulnerable to external threats and, therefore, seriously challenged in carrying out its mission.

Consider the following:

Since it is impossible to route public utility lines around a nearly 500-mile-long park, some 400 right-of-way crossings for power, communications, water and sewer lines are allowed by deeded easement or temporary permit. Overhead lines are objectionable because of their high visibility, while underground lines may impact archaeological sites, wetlands or critical plant or animal habitats. Ever-increasing area development means more and more requests for new utility crossings.

Over 100 private deeded access roads cross the Parkway at grade. Residential subdivision of former neighboring agricultural land results in multiple users of access roads that were originally intended for a single farm family. Private road connections result in traffic turning unexpectedly on or off the Parkway motor road. Private drives also stimulate nonconforming uses of neighboring lands resulting in changes to traditional Parkway views.

Approximately 160 public roads and highways intersect the Parkway, most of them at grade. Increased adjacent development results in demand for improved public roads, which, in turn, stimulates yet further development in an unending cycle. Improved, paved and widened intersecting roads alter the visitor's aesthetic experience, threaten traditional Parkway structures such as the classic stone arch bridges and result in more and higher speed traffic intersecting the Parkway motor road.

Diminished air quality in the region impairs distant views from the Parkway. Acid precipitation originating from sources far from Parkway boundaries, combined with other stress factors, may be killing trees at higher Parkway elevations.

Changing land use patterns result in loss of agricultural land along the Parkway and increased visual exposure to residential and commercial structures. As examples of these changes, in less than a decade, farmer-owned land in Western North Carolina has decreased by 22 percent, twice the state's average rate of decline, while private forest land has diminished by 16,000 acres.

Rapid urban growth, particularly in the Roanoke, Virginia area, seriously impacts Parkway views.

With fewer farmers remaining on neighboring lands, it is increasingly difficult to recruit or retain interested lessees to continue traditional farming practices on our 400 agricultural leases. Often Parkway neighbors find it more profitable to sell former agricultural land for residential or commercial developments than to continue farming.

Road building and timber removal, particularly clear-cutting, in close proximity to the Parkway can result in diminished visual qualities.

The Parkway has an estimated 4,000 private neighboring landowners scattered along approximately 1,000 miles of boundary. Many neighbors, either knowingly or unknowingly, trespass onto federal land with home construction, driveways and other developments. Individually, most encroachments are small; but collectively they represent a significant impact.

Lack of effective land use planning and poor development standards are creating many problems for local communities as well as for the Parkway. Nowadays, highly visible mountain tops and ridge lines are preferred building sites, often leaving the Parkway little opportunity to screen developments.

A final complicating factor concerns land acquisition. We have identified approximately 350 neighboring tracts of land, totaling over 8,000 acres, for acquisition, either of fee simple title or an easement, in order to eliminate hazardous private crossings or to protect outstanding vistas. Frequently, we are unable to purchase vital tracts even from a willing seller due to limited funding. Once critical lands are lost to subdivision, the likelihood of ever acquiring them diminishes greatly. If we are able to purchase the subdivided parcels at a later date, the total cost is much greater.

In view of these threats and challenges, it is clear that the Blue Ridge Parkway is extremely vulnerable to external forces over which it has only limited control or no control whatsoever. The full extent and potential impacts of these threats are not fully understood at present, but we feel we can safely make several predictions:

1. Regional growth and development will continue well into the next century.
2. With that growth will come more threats to Parkway views, as well as to our cultural and natural resources.
3. The Parkway will not acquire significant additional acreage or scenic easements to protect views.
4. Parkway visitation will continue to grow, attracted primarily by the scenery.

As we anticipate future developments, we must recognize that the days of park managers and staffs effectively standing alone in protecting a park from external threats is long gone. We believe our best chance for protecting the values that have made the Blue Ridge Parkway world-renowned lies in reaching out into the community for support and cooperation.

Such joint efforts seem especially appropriate on the Parkway. From our very beginning in the mid-1930s, the Parkway has served as a model for cooperative planning between the states and the federal government. This outreach effort sees us actively involved with more than a dozen different organizations, some public, some private and some quasi-public.

Parkway Superintendent and former Director of the National Park Service Gary Everhardt has provided the following Vision Statement to guide formulation of Parkway policy: "The Parkway has a dynamic relationship with its changing environment that requires all personnel to incorporate state-of-the-art techniques and management approaches while adhering to basic concepts and objectives."

In the spirit of this Vision Statement, we are continually seeking new opportunities to enter into mutual agreements to protect the Parkway. Several proposals are being implemented or are being planned. Among them:

- Presently, we are negotiating with the North Carolina and Virginia Departments of Transportation to ensure that improvements to secondary roads on Parkway land take into account National Park Service concerns regarding traffic safety, aesthetics of the Parkway driving experience and ensuring that natural and cultural resources are not impaired.

- We participate in the planning process for all major improvements to primary federal and state highways and interstates that intersect the Parkway. The possible eligibility of the Parkway for nomination to the National Registry of Historic Places gives the National Park Service considerable leverage in protecting Parkway values. As an example, historic Parkway bridges, most of which are of arched-masonry construction, must be left in place or else replaced by bridges true to traditional Parkway design concepts.

- The Parkway passes some 185 miles through national forest land. We cultivate a close working relationship with officials of the George Washington, Jefferson, Pisgah and Nantahala National Forests in order to review, in advance, proposed Forest Service timber cutting and other land management activities with potential impacts to the Parkway.

- We have contacted the commissioners or supervisors of each of the 29 counties touched by the Parkway and asked that they help protect Parkway values in their planning activities and enactment and enforcement of appropriate land use ordinances. We feel that local officials must look more seriously at the need for some land use controls, despite misgivings of many residents and real estate developers.

- To follow up the last point, a recent study commissioned by the Federal Highway Administration found that in 1987 the Blue Ridge Parkway was responsible for visitor expenditures of $1.3 billion in Virginia and North Carolina. While these expenditures suggests that the Parkway provides great economic benefit to nearby communities, the figure is generalized and subject to interpretation. In time, we hope to be able to estimate economic impacts along the Parkway on a county level. If successful, we will convince local government and business interests that the parkway is indeed a "goose" that lays many "golden eggs" in local communities and is well worth their efforts to help protect.

- We participate in Western North Carolina Tomorrow, a group comprised of political leaders, county planners federal agencies, private citizens, business leaders and other interests striving for optimal land use planning in rural counties. WNCT has expressed interest in serving as a link between the Parkway and local government and private interests to strengthen support for protecting Parkway values for the benefit of all.

- The Parkway is developing criteria and mapping critical viewsheds beyond Parkway boundaries to identify areas of vulnerability. Once we have identified our critical viewsheds, we can be more proactive and precise in approaching the Forest Service and other Parkway neighbors in defining our areas of greatest concern and cooperatively developing protective strategies.

- The National Park Service is developing a vehicle access plan. Development of this plan is a sizeable and long-range undertaking. It will include input from the Federal Highway Administration, state departments of transportation, and county and city governments. Implementation of the plan, once approved, will be very costly. However, once fully implemented, many at-grade intersections would be eliminated, the Parkway's "limited access" concept would become a reality, and many of our external threats would be greatly diminished.

- We are an active member of Southern Appalachian Man and the Biosphere Cooperative (SAMAB). Founded in

1988, SAMAB brings together organizations responsible for resource management and economic development to promote research, further understanding and encourage wise use of the natural resources of the region.
- The largest group sharing our concerns is a 42-year-old private sector organization known as the Blue Ridge Parkway Association, which counts 600 members in Virginia, North Carolina and Tennessee. Most members are involved with services, accommodations and attractions within the Parkway corridor.
- Increasingly, we receive encouraging expressions of support from land trust organizations, such as the Trust for Public Land and the Conservation Fund. Hopefully, we can strengthen our ties with such groups, who may be able to purchase critical tracts and hold them for us until we obtain acquisition funds.
- Both Virginia and North Carolina plan to include the Parkway in their respective Scenic Byways programs. Current plans call for the Parkway to serve as a spine, connecting a number of intersecting public roads that have high scenic qualities. As criteria and management plans are developed, the states should be able to enhance and expand their efforts to retain scenic qualities within and in the vicinity of the Parkway corridor.
- With our support and encouragement, private citizens from Virginia and North Carolina have joined forces to form Friends of the Blue Ridge Parkway. The goal of this new organization is to help Parkway management by raising funds for the protection of existing historic structures; to provide for construction and operation of visitor use facilities; to provide educational opportunities involving the history of the Parkway and the culture and geography of adjacent areas.
- We are working closely with Roanoke County planning officials, Friends of the Blue Ridge Parkway and other interested parties to identify and protect by land use controls those critical views in the Roanoke area that are at high risk due to urban expansion. We are greatly encouraged by the strong expressions of community support. We hope that through our mutual planning efforts Roanoke may continue to prosper while the Parkway corridor is afforded the highest possible level of protection.

These are examples of our partnerships and cooperative arrangements that have helped the Blue Ridge Parkway protect its resources and show promise for much greater mutual support in the future.

The challenges facing the Parkway are great, our future is uncertain and to a large extent protection of visual qualities will remain beyond our direct control. Future changes in regional land use and the resultant impacts may well dwarf anything we have experienced so far.

Of course, we must keep our concerns in some reasonable perspective. Change is inevitable, and we will not win every battle. But, we do have many friends, partners and supporters. We believe that orderly and appropriate adjacent development can be consistent with protecting National Park interests. Through careful cooperative planning, it is possible to enhance the visitor's experience and protect park resources while providing local economic development incentives. Further, adjacent developments often provide essential services for park visitors.

The historical record gives us some cause for optimism. Many regard the changes to Parkway views over the past half-century to be, on balance, very positive. Despite current concerns, the extensive overgrazing and poor timber harvesting practices early in the century left many scenes of devastation, now largely restored.

Also, we must realize that there is some subjectivity as to the impacts of changing land use. I have had the experience of observing with dismay some new, highly-visible adjacent development, then listening to a Parkway visitor's enthusiastic ravings about the spectacular Parkway views, all while viewing the changes to the traditional scene that I found unsettling. While we cannot be complaisant in the face of rapid change, much of the visual quality we cherish is in the eye of the beholder.

To conclude, the Blue Ridge Parkway's mission and goals statement directs us: "to take a leadership role in developing cooperative relationships and establishing public and private partnerships to protect and enhance park and regional resources and greatly expanding our state and local community outreach program."

We feel we have had some notable successes, but believe there is much more that can be done by further strengthening and expanding partnerships and co-operative relationship. Working alone, the National Park Service's accomplishments would be very limited.

Only by working together effectively with area public and private sector interests, we may see the Blue Ridge Parkway continue as a world class scenic resource into the 21st century. The Parkway is firmly committed to this partnership approach.

---

Jim Fox is a native of Western Pennsylvania. He has a B.S. degree in Zoology from Penn State and a M.S. degree in Resource Development from Michigan State. Mr. Fox has been a park ranger for 25 years, having worked at Grand Canyon, Yellowstone and Lassen Volcanic National Parks and at Glen Canyon National Recreation Area prior to coming to the Blue Ridge Parkway in 1984. He is the Parkway's land resource specialist, dealing with viewshed protection, land acquisition, scenic easements and rights-of-way.

# Perceived Tourism Impacts and Attitudes Toward Land-Use Controls in Communities Along the Blue Ridge Parkway

*Sharon Kashkin and Gene Brothers*

## INTRODUCTION

The Blue Ridge Parkway is a 477 mile scenic corridor which runs along the crests of the Appalachian Mountains from the Shenandoah National Park in Virginia to the Great Smoky Mountains National Park in North Carolina. Developed and maintained by the National Park Service (NPS), it is the longest scenic drive in the world. Conflicts between groups supporting land use regulations and owners of private lands adjacent to the parkway have arisen over the development of lands in ways that are considered by some to be incompatible with the scenic integrity of the parkway. The purpose of this study was to investigate and analyze some of these conflicts as they relate to generating tourism to communities along the parkway.

The success of the parkway in attracting visitors has enormously benefited the economies of adjacent communities. Studies of the economic impact of the Blue Ridge Parkway have demonstrated these positive effects of the parkway upon adjacent land values and property taxes. In 1987 (Southeastern Research Institute 1990) an analysis of visitor expenditures found that parkway visitors spent about $1.3 billion in the surrounding counties, generating approximately $98 million in tax revenues and supporting more than 26,500 regional jobs.

The original development of the parkway was made possible through resource protection techniques including land grants and scenic easements (Blue Ridge Parkway 1988; Keiter 1988; Futrell 1988). The intention of this protection was to provide a buffer zone to insulate and protect the parkway from non conforming development on privately owned adjacent lands (Davis 1970). As a result of its success in attracting tourists to this mountain region, land values have risen dramatically, creating a large demand for commercial development. In an attempt at protection, NPS officials have strictly enforced the property rights originally granted to the federal government by the states of North Carolina and Virginia. Consequently, opposition to the strict controls of land use regulations has mounted from private landowners who want to develop their lands (Davis 1970). In 1992, Scenic America (a national conservation organization dedicated to preserving and enhancing the scenic qualities of America's communities and countryside) recognized the Blue Ridge Parkway as one of America's ten most endangered scenic roads, threatened by regional air pollution, diminishing scenic vistas, and by commercial or residential development within the view sheds (Scenic America 1992). The need for a balance between the demand for non-conforming development along the parkway and the longing to protect and preserve the scenic landscapes that are the basis for the parkway's existence has become apparent.

The purpose of this study was to identify and analyze the conflicts between the Blue Ridge Parkway and other groups supporting land use controls and owners of private lands adjacent to the parkway in North Carolina. These conflicts are over the development of private lands for commercial purposes, generally related to tourism. Specifically, the study objectives were: 1) to determine community leaders' perceptions of impacts from tourism on the Blue Ridge Parkway, North Carolina; 2) to identify current tourism related development and perceptions of needed development in communities along the Blue Ridge Parkway, North Carolina; 3) to determine the relationship between perceptions of impacts from tourism on the Blue Ridge Parkway, North Carolina and the current level of tourism related development; 4) to determine current attitudes toward scenic resource protection techniques in communities along the Blue Ridge Parkway, North Carolina; and 5) to determine the relationship between perceptions of impacts from tourism on the Blue Ridge Parkway, North Carolina and attitudes toward scenic resource protection techniques.

Results from this study are important to the future protection of the Blue Ridge Parkway and to other parks and attractions which rely on visual resources. The results identify how important the protection of visual resources really are to leaders and citizens of host communities where tourism can have impacts on the local economy. Furthermore, the results could provide a basis for land use and planning decisions along the Blue Ridge Parkway and in other regions where tourism depends on the natural environment. Finally, this study could contribute to a general understanding of how tourism development is affecting our nation's scenic landscapes.

## LITERATURE REVIEW

Economic impact studies have traditionally received considerable attention in tourism literature. Such studies attempt to estimate the monetary effects of spending by tourists in a community, region or state as a result of direct or indirect spending. Past research has shown that tourism can become an important component of local economies. Sound economic decisions require information about the effects of economic growth or decline and the benefits and/or costs of alternative development strategies (Hastings & Brucker 1989). Numerous studies have been conducted which assess just how much economic effect parks have on host communities (Swanson 1969; Bergstrom, Cordell, Watson, & Ashley 1990; Makowski 1990; Cordell, Bergstrom, & Watson 1992; Stynes 1992; Williams, D. 1992). One of the concerns brought out in these studies is that the aggregate impacts may be considerable but they are not equitably distributed among all areas surrounding the parks. A few of the communities are benefiting economically from development and providing services to the visitors. Other communities are missing out on the benefits because of the lack of development even though they do provide the scenic beauty that attracts the visitors. The Blue Ridge Parkway serves visitors as a corridor rather than a destination, so the spending patterns and the economic impacts are likely to reflect spending at particular nodes along the corridor.

The tourism industry in the mountain region of North Carolina (Western North Carolina) has generated approximately $863 million in yearly sales, about 19,000 jobs and more than $200 million in annual payroll (United States Travel Data Center 1992). Three studies have attempted to estimate the value of economic benefits the Blue Ridge Parkway brings to adjacent communities (Williams & Knoeber 1979; Williams 1981; Southeastern Research Institute 1990). The studies that have been reviewed point out that the parkway has contributed to the growth in tourism and the increase in demand for tourism related commercial developments. The economic effects that visitors using the Blue Ridge

Parkway have on specific communities have not been studied to date. In lieu of a more complete study that would be able to estimate direct and indirect economic effects at the county level, this study investigated what community leaders perceived to be the relative economic impacts to their individual communities from tourism on the parkway. In order to do this, the perceptions and attitudes of host community residents as presented in the tourism research literature were reviewed.

Historically, the social impacts of tourism have not received as much attention as the economic impacts. Most impact studies have been restricted to studying economic impacts in a vacuum. With this in mind, several authors have attempted to assess the impacts tourism can have on the social structures of communities and more specifically to determine permanent residents' perceptions and attitudes about the presence of tourism in their communities.

Measurement of perceptions and attitudes of residents has been the focus of many tourism impact studies. Perceptions are the ways in which individuals translate sensory data into meaningful information that can be used and acted upon (Fridgen 1991). Attitudes are intellectual, emotional, and behavioral responses to events, things, and persons which people learn over time (Fridgen 1991). Measurements of perceptions and attitudes are often used in lieu of measuring actual tourism impacts, to determine community reactions to tourism development (Sethna 1979; Belisle & Hoy 1980; Duffield & Long 1981; Sheldon & Var 1984; Ross 1992; Murphy 1983). This type of research has revealed that perceptions of tourism impacts are negatively related to the distance a person lives from a tourist zone. In addition, positive resident attitudes are a function of the state of tourist development of an area, and are reflective of perceptions of the social, cultural, and physical impacts of tourism on the community and its environment. These studies revealed that negative social impacts, economic impacts, stereotyping of visitors, purchasing of second homes by foreigners, cultural exchange, and the ecological impacts of tourism were the issues most important to residents. In addition, lifelong residents and native speaking residents tended to be more sensitive to the impacts of tourism on their culture, while residents in high density areas were more inclined to appreciate the benefits and importance of tourism than those who had less contact with tourists.

Perceptions of the environmental impacts of tourism represent another recognized area of study. Scenic beauty has many faces and means different things to different people, depending on their interests. The same landscape can seem agreeable or ugly, fitting or unsuitable, to people of various backgrounds and differing tastes. Diverse opinions relating to landscape judgments are pertinent because they combine to form overall aesthetic judgment (Holmes 1979). Several studies have focused on how residents of tourism communities perceive environmental effects (Farrell 1979; Pizam 1978; Liu & Var 1986; Liu, Sheldon, & Var 1987). Results from these studies indicated that the impact of tourism on the environment is of universal concern. The value of incorporating residents' perceptions in the evaluation of the effects of tourism development was identified, along with the fact that these residents were highly aware of the important role of government planning in the long-term protection of the environment. Likewise, these studies confirmed the necessity of adopting a holistic approach to tourism planning, since issues on the environment are not perceived as being entirely distinct from economic and social ones.

Residents' perceptions of tourism related development encompass another related area of study. The effects of land use decisions have a greater influence on local residents than they have on visitors, due to the local residents' proximity to the area of concern. According to Knopp (1979), inconsistencies or apparent attempts to "kill the goose that laid the golden egg" may be explained by local residents' long term association with the rural or natural environment. Local residents often reach a point of saturation where they may have experienced enough of the natural scene and prefer the change associated with development. As a result, public controls are directed toward the status quo with respect to the natural environment. In an attempt to understand the factors associated with preferences for tourism development, studies have looked at local residents' support for various levels of development (Ahmed 1986; Allen, Long, Perdue, & Kieselback 1988; Long, Perdue, & Allen 1990; Belisle & Hoy 1980; Sheldon & Var 1984). These studies concluded that support for tourism strategies varies with different perceptions of the product benefits offered and the impacts of tourism on the destination, and that low to moderate levels of tourism development are beneficial to a community, but as development continues residents' perceptions tend to take a downward trend.

Relationships between residents' perceptions of tourism and their economic dependency on tourism represent another area important to the study of tourism on the Blue Ridge Parkway. Perceptions of economic impacts from tourism have been examined by several authors (Rothman 1978; Pizam 1978; Thomason, Crompton, & Kamp 1979; Murphy 1981; Davis, Allen, & Cosenza 1988; ). Host community residents are often economically dependent upon visitors and benefit from the services and facilities that cater to tourists. However, vacationers also affect many aspects of local residents' lives, causing them to curtail certain activities and causing deterioration of some parts of their communities. Furthermore, this line of research suggested that residents are primarily interested in the ways in which tourism can develop local amenity resources and in the ways it can provide additional income for the community. All segments of the local population are not affected in the same way by tourism. Some individuals derive enormous benefits from tourism, while others experience tourism's negative effects such as traffic congestion and higher prices. In general, local residents have a positive attitude toward the variety of commercial operations developed to accommodate visitors (Knopp 1979). There are two phases to tourism impacts: 1) what perceivers believe to be the case (a situation often underlying policy decision); and 2) the scientific monitoring of actual physical changes in the total environment (Liu, Sheldon, & Var 1987). The studies that have been reviewed demonstrate that perceived impacts of tourism can be used successfully in determining how residents regard the impacts of tourism on their communities without having to complete a study evaluating the actual impacts. Based on reviewed literature, this study proposes that community leaders' perceptions of impacts from tourism on the parkway can be used in lieu of measuring actual economic impacts. This perceived level of impacts should relate positively to the level of willingness among community residents and leaders to take measures to regulate and plan for tourism related land development along the parkway.

Impacts of tourism development on host communities can be broadly categorized as economic, social, or physical (Runyan & Wu 1979). Past studies of economic impact reflect the importance of tourism to rural communities and specifically the importance of the Blue Ridge Parkway to its adjacent communities. A review of social literature provides support for measuring perceptions and attitudes of residents and community leaders in addition to measuring actual tourism impacts to a host community. Literature related to conflicts in tourism development, policies, regulations and planning techniques illustrates what can and has been done to protect the parkway and other scenic resources from what many consider to be incompatible tourism related development. A review of the literature related to the research problem reinforces a belief in preserving our natural and visual resources as tourist attractions in and of themselves. This is the basis for protecting the lands around the Blue Ridge Parkway in order to maintain its integrity as a scenic resource.

This study attempted to determine community leaders' perceptions and attitudes toward tourism on the parkway. It attempted to determine current tourism related development and perceptions of needed development in communities along the Parkway. Finally, it examined past and present attitudes toward land use planning and the likely acceptance by private landowners of scenic resource protection techniques.

## METHODOLOGY

An on-site inventory was conducted of tourism related accommodations and facilities at eighty public road access exits on the parkway within North Carolina. This "windshield" type survey was conducted on main roads within a five mile radius of each exit. This included roads on both sides of the parkway. Items recorded in this inventory consisted of any type of facility that could potentially cater to a tourist. This list included: lodging facilities, campgrounds, food services, convenience stores, entertainment, attractions, recreation, transportation, variety stores, drug stores, and gift shops. After all exits had been inventoried, five classifications including: remote, fairly remote, small tourism area, small urban area, and large urban area were defined based on levels of tourism related development. Several criteria were considered in the definition of these five categories. First, the windshield inventory provided a representation of the entire distribution of development on lands along the parkway, within North Carolina. Second, natural breaks in development levels, ranging from rural to urban, were identified from the inventory. Third, and finally, the five categories of development were created based on the exit inventories, natural breaks in development, and expert opinions. A stratified sample of five exits was selected as sample sites. Criteria used in selecting the exits included: development level classifications, geographic distribution of exits along the parkway, Blue Ridge Parkway traffic count data for each exit, and the desire to have representative exits from each of the three larger development categories. Exits which fell in the remote or fairly remote categories were not chosen as sample sites due to the limited number of community representatives at these sites.

During the winter of 1993, representatives in twenty-two municipalities and eleven counties within twenty miles of each of the five chosen exits were sent questionnaires. The selection of this sampling "frame" was based on expert opinions. It was presumed that tourists will generally travel to communities up to twenty miles away from an exit and still return to the parkway. A total of two hundred and forty representatives were identified as potential respondents. One hundred fifty-five representatives answered survey questions, resulting in a response rate of 65%; the distribution of the type of respondents did not differ significantly from the sample distribution.

Due to the high costs and logistical difficulties that would be associated with sampling the actual landowners and general residents of the communities, the sample population chosen for this study is representative of leaders within the communities along the parkway. The objective here was to analyze the perceptions and attitudes of community leaders as they represent community residents. Representative leaders included: administrators, elected officials, business community representatives, planners, community development representatives, and other miscellaneous representatives. Due to the dissimilarity in sizes and populations of counties and municipalities, the variety of regional offices, and the difficulty in obtaining complete lists of all representatives at each exit, the numbers of representatives sampled at each exit were not equal.

The format and design of the questionnaire were influenced by the objectives of this study. The questionnaire consisted of twenty-four knowledge- and opinion-oriented inquiries. Section one of the questionnaire focused on the objective of determining community leaders' perceptions of impacts from tourism on the Blue Ridge Parkway. Questions were designed to explore two main areas: community leaders' perceptions of the economic impacts of tourism and the overall importance of tourism as an industry in their specific communities. Section two of the survey contained questions related to the objectives of identifying current tourism related development and perceptions of needed development and determining current attitudes toward land use controls in communities along the parkway. The third objective of this research involved relationships between questions related to objectives one and two, while objective five involved relationships between questions related to objectives one and four.

A pretest of the questionnaire was administered to specific groups whose responsibilities parallel those of the sample population. Surveys were distributed to the sample population using a modified Dillman technique (Dillman, 1978). An initial survey was mailed followed by a reminder postcard, a follow up survey and reminder letter, and a second reminder postcard, respectively.

One research question and one null hypothesis were derived from the five objectives of the study. They are as follows:

**Research Question**

Is there a positive relationship between community leaders' perceptions of impacts from tourism on the Blue Ridge Parkway and the current levels of tourism related development in communities along the parkway?

**Null Hypothesis**

There is no relationship between community leaders' perceptions of impacts from tourism on the Blue Ridge Parkway and the perceived level of acceptance of scenic resource protection techniques.

One-way analysis of variance (Computing Resource Center 1992, sec. 5s, p. 86-94; Agresti & Finlay 1986; chap. 13.1) was used to determine if statistically significant relationships existed between current levels of tourism related develop-

Table 1.
Summary by Exit of Perceptions of Impacts from Tourism on the Blue Ridge Parkway

| Impact Questions | Sample Exits Data presented as mean responses* | | | | | $F, p**$ |
|---|---|---|---|---|---|---|
| | NC 16 Jefferson /West Jefferson Area | US 321-221 Blowing Rock/ Boone Area | NC 226A Little Switzerland /Spruce Pine Area | US 70 Asheville Area | US 19 Maggie Valley/ Cherokee Area | |
| 1. Importance of the tourism industry to the economy of NC? | 1.4 (n=25) | 1.2 (n=42) | 1.1 (n=11) | 1.2 (n=25) | 1.4 (n=52) | $F = 1.90$ $p = .1009$ |
| 3. Importance of tourism to local communities' economies? | 3.4 (n=25) | 1.8 (n=41) | 3.1 (n=10) | 2.4 (n=23) | 2.0 (n=52) | $F = 9.85$ $p = .0000$ |
| 5. Importance of tourism as an employer in local communites? | 3.0 (n=24) | 1.8 (n=42) | 2.5 (n=10) | 2.2 (n=24) | 1.8 (n=52) | $F = 7.30$ $p = .0000$ |
| 9. Overall economic impact of parkway on local communities? | 2.0 (n=25) | 1.6 (n=42) | 1.7 (n=11) | 1.6 (n=24) | 1.6 (n=52) | $F = 2.40$ $p = .0527$ |
| 11. Importance of parkway to local communities' economies? | 2.8 (n=25) | 1.7 (n=42) | 1.6 (n=11) | 2.1 (n=24) | 2.0 (n=52) | $F = 5.25$ $p = .0006$ |
| 13. Percentage of tourism that comes from Parkway? | 1.7 (n=25) | 2.2 (n=41) | 2.8 (n=11) | 2.6 (n=25) | 1.7 (n=52) | $F = 5.09$ $p = .0008$ |

* Mean responses calculated for categories 1-5, category 6, Not Sure/Don't Know, not included.
** Highlighted p values represent statistically significant differences at .05 level.

ment and perceptions of impacts from tourism (research question). This analysis allowed for the determination of significant differences between responses of specific groups. In this case, the groups were the five exits, which represent three development levels. In addition, the Bonferroni multiple comparison test was used to determine more specifically where the differences existed (Computing Resource Center 1992; sec. 5s, p. 86-94).

Pearson correlations were calculated to measure the degree of linear association between community attitudes toward scenic resource protection techniques and perceived impacts from tourism on the parkway (null hypothesis).

## RESULTS

The first objective of this study was: To determine community leaders' perceptions of impacts from tourism on the Blue Ridge

Parkway, North Carolina. Community leaders' perceptions for the "impact" questions are summarized in Table 1 by parkway exit. Objective three of this study was to look at the relationship between the current level of tourism related development and community leaders' perceptions of impacts from tourism on the Blue Ridge Parkway. To do this, comparisons were made for these "impacts," using Oneway Analysis of Variance. Each of the five sample exits was categorized into one of three development levels (US 70=Large Urban Area; NC 226A=Small Urban Area; US 321-221= Small Urban Area; NC 16=Small Tourist Area; and US 19=Small Tourist Area). The objective here was to determine whether there were statistically significant differences in the perceptions and attitudes of community leaders representing three different development levels, regarding impacts of tourism on the parkway. As summarized in Table 1, statistically significant differences between exits were found for several questions. The mean responses by exit for each question is presented, along with the $F$-statistic and $p$- value for each analysis.

When community representatives were asked how important they felt tourism is to the economy of North Carolina, no differences were found among the exit groups or development levels. Almost 100% felt it was important, or very important. Conversely, significant differences were found between the exits in regard to their perceptions of the importance of tourism to their specific communities as an industry and as an employer. Respondents were asked, "How important do you feel the tourism industry is to your community's economy?" Statistically significant differences were found among representatives from the exits; however, there was no correlation between the differences and level of current development.

Statistically significant differences in perceptions of the importance of tourism as an employer in specific communities were also found. Respondents were asked, "How important is tourism as an employer in your community?" As with the importance of tourism as an industry, the majority of differences in responses did not vary with development levels. Differences were also found among the exits in their perceptions of how important the parkway is to their communities' economies and in their perceptions of the percentage of tourism in their communities that comes from travel on the parkway. These differences did not correlate with current development level. Therefore, there is not sufficient evidence to assume that perceptions differ positively by development level.

When community officials were asked if they felt the positive benefits gained from the parkway outweigh the negative costs to their community, 91% of the respondents said yes. No statistically significant differences were found among the development levels.

The research question for this study asked whether a positive relationship existed between perceived levels of impacts from tourism on the parkway and the current levels of tourism related developed. In some cases, perceptions did relate positively with development levels. In other cases, differences were noted between exits, but these differences did not have a positive relationship with level of development. Therefore, while this analysis provided partial support, it is not sufficient to conclude that a positive relationship exists between perceptions of impacts from tourism on the parkway and the current level of tourism related development.

Table 2.
Summary by Exit of Community Leaders' Opinions of
Current Tourism-Related Development

| Facility/ Attraction | Sample Exits Data presented as mean responses* | | | | | $F, p**$ |
|---|---|---|---|---|---|---|
| | NC 16 Jefferson /West Jefferson Area | US 321-221 Blowing Rock/ Boone Area | NC 226A Little Switzer-land /Spruce Pine Area | US 70 Asheville Area | US 19 Maggie Valley/ Cherokee Area | |
| **Lodging Facilities** | | | | | | |
| Hotels (< 50 units) | 2.25 (n=24) | 2.6 (n=36) | 2.0 (n=10) | 2.6 (n=16) | 2.6 (n=49) | $F = 2.16$ $p = .0770$ |
| Hotels (>=50 units) | 2.6 (n=16) | 2.5 (n=31) | 2.0 (n=5) | 2.7 (n=15) | 2.2 (n=42) | $F = 1.47$ $p = .2178$ |
| Bed & Breakfasts | 2.3 (n=20) | 2.5 (n=39) | 2.2 (n=10) | 2.3 (n=22) | 2.2 (n=49) | $F = 0.78$ $p = .5382$ |
| Campgrounds | 2.3 (n=22) | 2.4 (n=38) | 2.5 (n=11) | 2.1 (n=19) | 2.6 (n=45) | $F = 1.74$ $p = .1456$ |
| Youth Camps | 1.8 (n=12) | 2.4 (n=30) | 2.3 (n=3) | 2.6 (n=16) | 2.1 (n=36) | $F = 2.45$ $p = .0514$ |
| Resorts | 2.11 (n=9) | 2.7 (n=31) | 2.0 (n=4) | 2.11 (n=17) | 2.2 (n=45) | $F = 2.15$ $p = .0798$ |
| Time-Share Condominiums | 2.0 (n=9) | 3.8 (n=26) | 3.0 (n=3) | 3.3 (n=7) | 2.8 (n=32) | $F = 6.17$ $p = .0003$ |
| **Recreation/Attractions** | | | | | | |
| Theme Parks | 1.0 (n=3) | 2.7 (n=27) | 3.0 (n=2) | 3.9 (n=7) | 2.7 (n=39) | $F = 4.80$ $p = .0017$ |
| Miniature Golf Courses | 2.7 (n=10) | 2.5 (n=31) | 2.3 (n=6) | 2.7 (n=9) | 2.5 (n=38) | $F = 0.22$ $p = .9283$ |
| Water Parks | 2.0 (n=5) | 2.5 (n=15) | 3.0 (n=3) | 2.8 (n=4) | 2.4 (n=28) | $F = 0.58$ $p = .6808$ |
| Night Clubs | 2.6 (n=12) | 3.0 (n=23) | 3.0 (n=3) | 3.11 (n=9) | 2.7 (n=41) | $F = 0.47$ $p = .7588$ |
| White Water Sports | 2.6 (n=13) | 2.6 (n=30) | 2.4 (n=8) | 2.3 (n=12) | 2.6 (n=35) | $F = .036$ $p = .8362$ |
| Hiking Trails | 2.3 (n=21) | 2.3 (n=36) | 1.9 (n=11) | 2.1 (n=19) | 2.5 (n=45) | $F = 2.12$ $p = .0825$ |
| Natural Resource/ Recreation Areas | 2.2 (n=19) | 2.1 (n=36) | 1.8 (n=8) | 2.1 (n=20) | 2.0 (n=43) | $F = 0.52$ $p = .7192$ |
| Museums | 1.8 (n=13) | 2.0 (n=29) | 2.3 (n=10) | 2.2 (n=19) | 1.9 (n=43) | $F = 1.28$ $p = .2811$ |
| Historic Sites | 2.1 (n=16) | 2.0 (n=35) | 2.3 (n=10) | 2.2 (n=17) | 1.9 (n=44) | $F = 1.00$ $p = .4121$ |

\* (1=Not Nearly Enough; 2=Need A Little More; 3=Just Right; 4=A Little More Than Needed; 5=Way too Many)
\*\* Highlighted values represent statistically significant differences at .05 level of significance.

Objective 2 for this study relates to identifying current tourism related development and perceptions of needed development in communities along the Blue Ridge Parkway, North Carolina. Community leaders' perceptions of needed development along the parkway were measured by two questions. The questions were designed to determine community leaders' opinions concerning the current level of development of thirty-one different types of tourism related facilities or

Table 2. *continued*
Summary by Exit of Community Leaders' Opinions of
Current Tourism-Related Development

Sample Exits
Data presented as mean responses*

| Facility/ Attraction | NC 16 Jefferson /West Jefferson Area | US 321-221 Blowing Rock/ Boone Area | NC 226A Little Switzer-land /Spruce Pine Area | US 70 Asheville Area | US 19 Maggie Valley/ Cherokee Area | $F, p^{**}$ |
|---|---|---|---|---|---|---|
| **Recreation/Attractions - Continued** | | | | | | |
| Sports Facilities | 2.2 (n=16) | 2.2 (n=35) | 2.0 (n=7) | 2.0 (n=18) | 2.1 (n=44) | $F = 0.19$ $p = .9410$ |
| Theaters | 2.2 (n=14) | 2.6 (n=34) | 1.7 (n=9) | 2.5 (n=14) | 1.8 (n=44) | $F = 5.74$ $p = .0003$ |
| Cultural/Ethnic Attractions | 2.1 (n=15) | 1.9 (n=30) | 1.8 (n=8) | 2.2 (n=16) | 1.8 (n=42) | $F = 0.80$ $p = .5278$ |
| Special Events | 2.1 (n=15) | 2.1 (n=32) | 1.9 (n=8) | 2.2 (n=16) | 2.1 (n=45) | $F = 0.16$ $p = .9578$ |
| Golf Courses | 2.7 (n=23) | 2.2 (n=41) | 2.0 (n=9) | 2.7 (n=19) | 2.4 (n=42) | $F = 2.22$ $p = .0703$ |
| Ski Slopes | 2.4 (n=7) | 2.9 (n=31) | 2.6 (n=7) | 2.8 (n=9) | 2.6 (n=38) | $F = 0.95$ $p = .4396$ |
| Go Cart Tracks | 2.7 (n=7) | 3.4 (n=27) | 3.0 (n=2) | 4.2 (n=5) | 3.3 (n=34) | $F = 1.77$ $p = .1445$ |
| **Service Facilities** | | | | | | |
| Gas Stations | 3.0 (n=23) | 3.1 (n=40) | 2.9 (n=11) | 3.1 (n=19) | 2.9 (n=47) | $F = 0.46$ $p = .7658$ |
| Fast Food Restaurants | 2.8 (n=22) | 3.3 (n=39) | 3.2 (n=9) | 3.2 (n=19) | 3.0 (n=46) | $F = 1.35$ $p = .2549$ |
| Full Service Restaurants | 2.1 (n=22) | 2.3 (n=39) | 2.1 (n=11) | 2.5 (n=20) | 2.0 (n=46) | $F = 1.3$ $p = .2746$ |
| Convenience Stores | 3.1 (n=23) | 3.5 (n=41) | 3.3 (n=11) | 3.2 (n=19) | 3.1 (n=47) | $F = 1.89$ $p = .1154$ |
| **Shopping Facilities** | | | | | | |
| Gift Shops | 2.8 (n=20) | 3.0 (n=34) | 2.1 (n=10) | 2.9 (n=16) | 3.1 (n=45) | $F = 3.13$ $p = .0174$ |
| Antique Shops | 2.7 (n=23) | 2.9 (n=37) | 2.0 (n=9) | 2.9 (n=18) | 2.9 (n=47) | $F = 2.35$ $p = .0578$ |
| Local Craft Shops | 2.7 (n=23) | 2.8 (n=39) | 2.4 (n=10) | 2.6 (n=20) | 2.7 (n=47) | $F = .45$ $p = .7720$ |
| Convention Facilities | 2.25 (n=8) | 2.3 (n=28) | 2.0 (n=3) | 2.4 (n=17) | 1.9 (n=37) | $F = 1.45$ $p = .2237$ |

*(1=Not Nearly Enough; 2=Need A Little More; 3=Just Right; 4=A Little More Than Needed; 5=Way too Many)
** Highlighted values represent statistically significant differences at .05 level of significance.

attractions. Respondents were first asked on a five point scale (1=Not Nearly Enough; 2=Need a little More; 3=Just Right; 4=A Little More Needed; 5=Way Too Many) to indicate their opinions concerning the level of development for those attractions or facilities which are currently in their community or county. Results are compared by exit for each of the related facilities and attractions using Analysis of Variance (Table 2).

Facilities and attractions were grouped

into five main categories including: *lodging facilities, service facilities, recreation/attractions, shopping,* and *convention facilities.* A general trend prevailed among the community leaders' opinions, with the majority of responses falling in the "Need a Little More" and "Just Right" categories.

Statistically significant differences between the exit groups were found only in four out of thirty-one possibilities. These included current levels of time-share condominiums, theme parks, theaters, and gift shops. In the case of time-share condominiums, significant differences were found between representatives from the exits at US 321-221 and both NC 16 and US 19. In the overall sample response, over 45% said the current development is just right. Representatives from the exit at US 321-221 felt there were way too many time-share condominiums, with over 96% of the response falling between the "Just Right" and "Way too Many" categories. In comparison, responses from NC 16 were skewed in the opposite direction, with 100% the responses falling equally between the "Not Nearly Enough" and "Just Right" categories. In addition, over 50% of the representatives at US 19 said it is just right, while another 31% said they need more. While the responses at NC 226A and US 70 were not found to be significantly different, it should be noted that responses at these exits were very split among the five response categories (Table 2).

When respondents were asked to rate the current development of theme parks, statistically significant differences were also found among the exits (Table 2). The average response for the entire sample was "Need a Little More" to "Just Right" (2.7), which accounted for over 69% of the responses. Significant differences were noted between NC 226A and US 19 and between US 70 and NC 16.

Statistically significant differences were also found between certain exits regarding the current development of theaters. As presented in Table 2, differences in responses were found between US 321-221, in which over 65% of the representatives said "Just Right" and both NC 226A and US 19. In the case of NC 226A, over 55% said there are "Not Nearly Enough" theaters, with the remaining 44% split between "Need a Little More" and "Just Right." Representatives at US 19 were skewed more toward "Not Nearly Enough" (38.6%), and "Need a Little More" (40.9%).

Current development of gift shops makes up the last category in which statistically significant differences were also found between certain exits. Over 50% of the respondents felt that the current development of gift shops is "Just Right," with an additional 22% saying they "Need a Little More." Statistically significant differences in responses were found between US 226A and US 19. The majority of responses (90%) at US 226A ranged from "Not Nearly Enough" to "Just Right." In comparison, response at US 19 followed a more normal distribution, with over 50% saying development of gift shops is "Just Right."

The second question relating to current types of development probed further into community leaders' opinions on tourism related development. Using the same listing of tourism related facilities or attractions, respondents were asked to indicate the three attractions or facilities they would MOST LIKE to see developed in their community in the future with a 1, 2, and 3 ranking. Respondents were then asked to indicate the three attractions or facilities they would LEAST LIKE to see developed, ranking them as A, B, and C. During data analysis, the A, B, and C rankings were recoded as 29, 30, and 31. Responses for each facility or attraction were then totaled and averaged to achieve an overall ranking for each item. As presented in Table 3, the top five facilities or attractions that community leaders would MOST LIKE to see developed in their communities included: #1-Natural Resource/Recreation Areas; #2-Youth Camps; #3-Historic Sites; #4-Full Service Restaurants; and #5-Golf Courses (Note: Mean scores in Table 3 are mean rank scores). The five facilities or attractions that community leaders would LEAST LIKE to see developed included: Time Share Condominiums, Night Clubs, Go Cart Tracks, Convenience Stores, and Gas Stations, ranked 27-31, respectively. These results show that community representatives feel that developments should be complimentary to the parkway.

Objective four of this study was to determine current attitudes toward scenic resource protection techniques in com-

Table 3.
Opinion Rankings for Desired Types of Tourism Development

| Facility/Attraction | Mean Rank Score | Ranking |
|---|---|---|
| Natural Resource/Recreation Areas | 1.62 | 1 |
| Youth Camps | 2.23 | 2 |
| Historic Sites | 2.47 | 3 |
| Full Service Restaurants | 3.50 | 4 |
| Golf Courses | 3.63 | 5 |
| Campgrounds | 3.92 | 6 |
| Bed and Breakfasts | 4.42 | 7 |
| Special Events | 4.60 | 8 |
| Cultural/Ethnic Attractions | 4.67 | 9 |
| Theaters | 4.95 | 10 |
| Sports Facilities | 5.30 | 11 |
| Museums | 5.69 | 12 |
| Convention Centers | 6.09 | 13 |
| Hotels with less than 50 units | 9.97 | 14 |
| Local Craft Shops | 11.58 | 15 |
| Resorts | 11.59 | 16 |
| Hotels with 50 or more units | 12.14 | 17 |
| Hiking Trails | 16.13 | 18 |
| White Water Sports | 16.13 | 18 |
| Ski Slopes | 18.50 | 20 |
| Gift Shops | 20.78 | 21 |
| Miniature Golf Courses | 21.30 | 22 |
| Water Parks | 25.70 | 23 |
| Antique Shops | 25.86 | 24 |
| Theme Parks | 26.77 | 25 |
| Fast Food Restaurants | 27.65 | 26 |
| Time Share Condominiums | 28.96 | 27 |
| Night Clubs | 29.26 | 28 |
| Go Cart Tracks | 29.68 | 29 |
| Convenience Stores | 29.70 | 30 |
| Gas Stations | 29.88 | 31 |

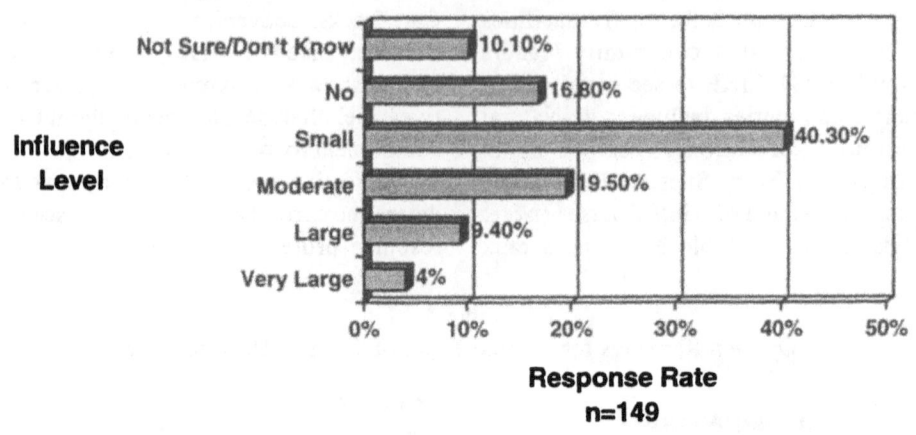

Figure 1. Influence of Parkway's Presence on Past Land-Use and Development Decisions
(Data presented as percent of total response.)

munities along the Blue Ridge Parkway, North Carolina. Once it was determined how important community leaders perceived tourism and the Blue Ridge Parkway to be to their communities, their attitudes toward current and potential scenic resource protection techniques along the parkway were measured using two groups of questions. The first set of questions dealt with present and future influences of the parkway on community development decisions. The second set of questions dealt more specifically with the likely acceptance by landowners of certain types of scenic resource protection techniques. Analysis of these data are presented first for the overall sample and then by each exit group in order to make comparisons by development levels.

Several questions were designed to determine how community leaders felt about various land use regulations and development decisions on lands along the parkway. One question was designed to determine how much of an influence the parkway's presence has had on land use and development decisions in their county. Respondents were asked, on a scale of 1 to 6 (1=Very Large Influence; 2=Large Influence; 3=Moderate Influence; 4=Small Influence; 5=No Influence; 6=Not Sure/Don't Know), how much of an influence the presence of the parkway has had on land use and development decisions in their county. Of one hundred and forty-nine respondents, just over 40% said it has had a small influence, while 19.5% said it has had only a moderate influence. These were followed by 17% that said it had no influence. Only 13% of the respondents felt the parkway's presence has had a large or very large influence on land use and development decisions.

In order to determine community leaders' opinions about what role the parkway should play in future development decisions, they were asked, on a scale of 1 to 5, (1=Very Large Role; 2=Large Role; 3=Moderate Role; 4=Small Role; 5=No Role), "What role do you feel tourism from the parkway should play in future development in your community?" Of 154 responses, over 40% said they felt tourism should play a large role in the future development of their community. An additional 19% said it should play a very large role and 30% said it should play a moderate role. Conversely, only 10% of the respondents said tourism should play a small role or no role in the future development of their community.

An important conclusion can be drawn from these two questions. Responses suggest that while most representatives felt that the parkway's presence has had a minimal influence on past land development decisions within their communities, the majority also felt it should play at least a moderate role in future development.

Another two questions were designed to determine if community leaders felt that current and future land uses along the parkway are important issues that should be dealt with by government officials. These land uses include such things as: farming, timber harvesting, housing developments, and commercial establishments. The first of these two questions attempted to determine how leaders felt about "current" land uses. Of 151 respondents, over 74% said yes, that they felt current land uses along the parkway are important issues and that they should be dealt with by government officials. Conversely, 17.2% said no, and 8.6% were not sure or did not know. Those respondents who said yes were given the option to indicate at what levels of government they felt these "current" issues should be handled. Of the 112 respondents who said yes, 70 indicated that these issues should be handled at the federal level, while 77 respondents said state level, 69 officials supported county government; and 37 indicated municipal level (Table 4, totals are greater than 112 due to multiple responses).

When asked to indicate if they felt "future" land use changes along the parkway were important issues that should be dealt with by government officials, a similar pattern emerged. Of 150 responses, 86% said yes, while only 8% said no and 6% were not sure or did not know. In addition, when asked to indicate at what level these "future" issues should be handled, 87 respondents said federal government, 93 state level, 83 county level, and 43 said municipal (Table 4, totals are greater than 150 due to multiple responses).

In addition to determining community leaders' opinions about government intervention in land use issues, respondents

Figure 2. Community Leaders' Opinions Regarding the Role Tourism Should Play in the Future Development of their Communities (Data presented as percent of total responses.)

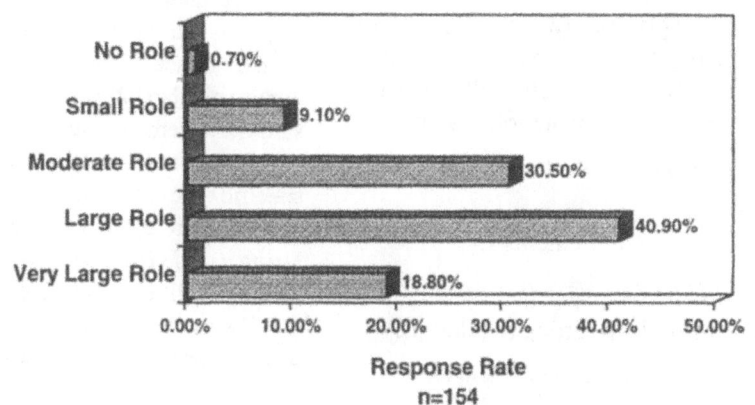

Table 4.
Are Current or Future Land Uses Important Issues
that Should be Dealt with by Government Officials?

| Responses | Current Uses (% of Response) (n=151) | Future Changes (% of Response) (n=150) |
|---|---|---|
| Yes | 74.2% | 86.0% |
| No | 17.2% | 8.0% |
| Not Sure/Don't Know | 8.6% | 6.0% |
| **If Yes, What Level?** | % of Responses (253 responses)* | % of Responses (306 responses)* |
| Federal Level | 28.0% | 28.0% |
| State Level | 30.0% | 30.0% |
| County Level | 27.0% | 27.0% |
| Municipal Level | 15.0% | 15.0% |

* Respondents had opportunity to check all levels of government that applied.

were asked, "Do you believe that it is important for your community to have direct input and involvement in creating policies which deal with land use and development along the parkway?" A majority (79%) said yes, while only 16% said no, and 5% were unsure.

Respondents were also asked if they were aware of any land development regulations which deal with development along the parkway that had been passed or were being negotiated in their community. An overwhelming 70% of respondents said No, they were not aware of any land development regulations. Only 14% said Yes, while 17% said they were not sure or did not know. Those respondents who did reply Yes (21) were given the opportunity to openly explain the nature of these regulations. The following is a summary of the explanations listed:

- Watershed Protection/Water Quality Act
- Set back requirements
- Ridge law
- Timber clear-cutting regulations
- Sign controls and ordinances
- View preservation
- Community officials opposing clear-cutting along parkway
- Local codes regulating property adjacent to parkway
- Revisions to city ordinances to protect parkway
- Encouragement of structures of a particular appearance within the view-sheds by parkway

Blue Ridge Parkway (NPS) officials have stated that they feel strongly that it is important to have local citizen involvement in the planning and negotiations over land development issues along the parkway. When asked whether local officials have seen evidence of this, 47% of the respondents said No, 28% said Yes, and 25% said they were not sure or did not know.

One final question was related to specific types of scenic resource protection tools that are often used by communities. Using a scale from 0 to 5 (0=Don't Know; 1=Very Unlikely; 2=Unlikely; 3=Neutral; 4=Likely; 5=Very Likely), respondents were asked to indicate how likely it would be for landowners in their community to accept sixteen different types of land use control techniques. These techniques are categorized as: Land Acquisition Approaches, Land Transfer Controls, Land Use Controls, Land Development Controls, Tax Incentives, Planning, Sign Controls, View Preservation Ordinances, and Voluntary Approaches.

As presented in Table 5, two main patterns of probable acceptance emerged. Over 50% of the respondents rated Land Acquisition Techniques (52%) and Land Transfer Controls (61%) as "Very Unlikely" to "Unlikely" to be accepted. With very few exceptions, the remaining categories of scenic resource protection tools were skewed toward "Likely" to "Very Likely" acceptance. In most cases, Land Use Controls were rated as "Neutral" to "Likely" over 58% of the time (Easements 59%, Scenic Highway Designation 60%, Agricultural Districts 67%). Exceptions were noted with Zoning Ordinances which were skewed toward "Very Unlikely" and "Unlikely" by 60% of the respondents.

Responses in the Land Development Controls category were somewhat varied. Subdivision Districts were rated most often (56% of the time) as "Neutral" to "Likely." Cluster Development was more spread out between "Unlikely" to "Likely," which accounted for 66% of the response. Conversely, Development Moratorium was skewed very far toward "Very Unlikely" and "Unlikely," which accounted for 64% of the response.

Responses for the majority of the remaining scenic resource protection tools were much more uniform. In five out of seven cases, acceptance ratings fell into "Neutral" to "Likely" at least 55% of the time. These included Tax Incentives 55%, Comprehensive Planning 59%, Site Plan Reviews 70%, View Protection Ordinances 59%, and Tree Protection Ordinances 59%.

Responses for Sign Controls were a bit more spread out to include "Unlikely," making the three categories account for 76% of the response. Voluntary Approaches shifted slightly in the other direction to include "Very Likely," making the three categories account for 81% of the responses.

The preceding section offered a descriptive analysis of response rates to questions related to land development issues and scenic resource protection techniques in communities along the parkway. In this section, the sample population will be broken down by exit group. Comparisons between exits will determined using analysis of variance. The Pearson correlation (Sommer & Sommer 1980, p. 219; Computing Resource Center 1992, sec. 5s, p. 204-208) was also used in the comparative analysis as a measure of association to determine what type of relationship, if any, exists between perceived impacts and likely acceptance of scenic resource protection techniques.

The group of questions used to examine attitudes toward scenic resource protection techniques were categorized and comparisons were made by category only. In order to accomplish this, an index was computed for those categories which included more than one land use control technique. A mean score was computed for each technique by exit. Oneway analysis of variance was used to determine if statistically significant differences existed among the exits in their likely acceptance of each of the nine technique categories. As summarized in Table 6, statistically significant differences among the exits were found in seven of nine categories, excluding only tax incentives and voluntary approaches.

Mean scores for the nine technique categories where statistically significant differences between exits occurred are

Table 5.
Likelihood of Acceptance of Scenic Resource Protection Techniques
in Communities Along the Blue Ridge Parkway

**Response Categories**
Data presented as percent of total response*

| Techniques | Don't Know 0 | Very Unlikely 1 | Unlikely 2 | Neutral 3 | Likely 4 | Very Likely 5 | Response Rate/Mean Response (1-5)** |
|---|---|---|---|---|---|---|---|
| **Land Acquisition** | 12.4% | 26.9% | 24.8% | 10.3% | 21.4% | 4.1% | 127 / 2.4 |
| **Land Transfer Controls** | 19.0% | 28.2% | 32.4% | 12.0% | 4.9% | 3.5% | 115 / 2.1 |
| **Land Use Controls** | | | | | | | |
| Scenic Easements | 5.5% | 10.3% | 17.9% | 25.5% | 33.1% | 7.6% | 137 / 3.1 |
| Scenic Hwy. Zoning | 6.2% | 13.8% | 17.9% | 29.7% | 26.2% | 6.2% | 136 / 2.9 |
| Agricultural Districts | 6.3% | 7.7% | 11.2% | 25.9% | 41.3% | 7.7% | 134 / 3.3 |
| Zoning Ordinances | 2.7% | 35.9% | 24.1% | 11.0% | 17.2% | 9.0% | 145 / 2.3 |
| **Land Develop. Controls** | | | | | | | |
| Subdivision Districts | 3.5% | 12.4% | 14.5% | 17.9% | 37.9% | 13.8% | 140 / 3.3 |
| Cluster Development | 12.5% | 15.3% | 17.4% | 30.6% | 18.1% | 6.3% | 126 / 2.8 |
| Development Moratorium | 7.9% | 36.0% | 28.1% | 15.1% | 6.5% | 6.5% | 128 / 2.1 |
| **Tax Incentives** | 9.7% | 10.4% | 16.7% | 20.8% | 34.7% | 7.6% | 130 / 3.1 |
| **Planning** | | | | | | | |
| Comprehensive Plans | 12.1% | 7.9% | 15.0% | 30.0% | 29.3% | 5.7% | 123 / 3.1 |
| Site Plan Reviews | 6.4% | 7.8% | 9.9% | 30.5% | 39.0% | 6.4% | 132 / 3.2 |
| Sign Controls | 2.8% | 6.9% | 16.7% | 14.6% | 45.1% | 13.9% | 140 / 3.4 |
| **View Protection** | | | | | | | |
| View Preserv. Ordinances | 5.5% | 8.3% | 16.6% | 24.1% | 35.2% | 10.3% | 137 / 3.2 |
| Tree Protection Ordinances | 4.8% | 11.0% | 14.4% | 16.4% | 42.5% | 11.0% | 139 / 3.3 |
| **Voluntary Approaches** | 4.8% | 8.2% | 6.2% | 14.4% | 53.4% | 13.0% | 139 / 3.6 |

\* Bold values highlight patterns of majority of responses.
\*\* Mean values and response rates calculated for responses to categories 1-5.

highlighed in Table 6. In every case, statistically significant differences were found between US 321-221 and another exit. In the case of Land Acquisition Techniques, differences were found between respondents at US 321-221 and US 226A. Differences in responses to Land Transfer Controls were found between US 321-221 and NC 16. Differences were also found between these same exits for Land Use Control Techniques. In both cases, statistically significant differences were not found between any other exits. Differences in responses to View Protection ordinances were found between US 321-221 and NC 19. In the cases of Land Development Controls and Planning Techniques, responses from representatives at US 321-221 differed once again from NC 16 and NC 19. For Sign Controls, US 321-221 differed from NC 19 and US 226A. US 70 had no responses that were significantly different from other exits. In addition, no differences in responses were found among exits for Tax Incentives or Voluntary Approaches.

Objective five of this study was to determine if a positive relationship exists between perceived impacts from tourism on the parkway and attitudes toward scenic resource protection techniques. This objective relates to the null hypothesis of this study, as stated in the Methods section. Pearson correlations were used to measure the level of linear association between these variables (Sommer & Sommer 1980, p. 219; Agresti and Finlay 1986, sec. 9.3). Four indexes, representing the total sample and each of the three tourism development levels, were created for perceived impacts using questions in the first section of the questionnaire. These questions all related to community leaders' perceptions of impacts to their communities from tourism on the parkway. In order to determine the nature of the relationships, the indexes for perceived tourism impacts were correlated against the nine categories of scenic resource protection techniques.

Pearson correlations, presented in Table 7, for the total sample ranged from .0338 for Voluntary Approaches and .3258 for Land Development Controls. Interpretation of this statistic reveals that, in the strongest case, only 10.6% ($.3258^2$) of the variability in attitudes toward scenic resource protection techniques can be explained by the perceptions of impacts from the parkway. Moreover, when the responses are broken down by development levels, the relationships were no stronger. In some cases, the relationships were even found to be negative. Therefore, the null hypothesis that no relationship exists between perceptions of impacts from tourism on the Blue Ridge Parkway and attitudes toward land use controls was not rejected.

## CONCLUSIONS

Results from this study are important to the future protection of the Blue Ridge Parkway and to other parks and attractions

Table 6.
Likely Acceptance of Scenic Resource Protection Techniques by Exit

| Technique Categories | Mean Response by Exit ** | | | | | $F, p$*** |
|---|---|---|---|---|---|---|
| | NC 16 | US 19 | US 321-221 | NC 226A | US 70 | |
| Land Acquisition | 1.8 (n=22) | 2.3 (n=44) | <u>3.2</u> (n=31) | *2.0 (n=10) | 2.7 (n=20-) | $F = 5.16$ $p = .0007$ |
| Land Transfer Controls | *1.6 (n=19) | 1.9 (n=39) | <u>2.5</u> (n=29) | 1.8 (n=10) | 2.2 (n=18) | $F = 2.73$ $p = .0326$ |
| Land Use Controls | *2.7 (n=20) | 2.6 (n=42) | <u>3.6</u> (n=32) | 2.33 (n=9) | 3.1 (n=18) | $F = 9.92$ $p = .0000$ |
| Land Development Controls | *2.2 (n=19) | *2.5 (n=38) | <u>3.4</u> (n=33) | 2.5 (n=10) | 2.8 (n=16) | $F = 6.93$ $p = .0000$ |
| Tax Incentives | 2.6 (n=21) | 3.1 (n=44) | 3.5 (n=37) | 3.3 (n=10) | 3.1 (n=18) | $F = 1.86$ $p = .1219$ |
| Planning | *2.8 (n=20) | *2.9 (n=44) | <u>3.8</u> (n=34) | 3.0 (n=9) | 3.4 (n=15) | $F = 6.55$ $p = .0000$ |
| Sign Controls | 3.5 (n=23) | *3.0 (n=47) | <u>4.1</u> (n=39) | *2.7 (n=10) | 3.5 (n=21) | $F = 6.8$ $p = .0000$ |
| View Protection | 3.1 (n=21) | *3.0 (n=46) | <u>3.8</u> (n=36) | 3.0 (n=11) | 3.3 (n-19) | $F = 3.70$ $p = .0070$ |
| Voluntary Approaches | 3.5 (n=22) | 3.3 (n=48) | 3.9 (n=37) | 3.7 (n=11) | 3.6 (n=21) | $F = 1.77$ $p = .1386$ |

* Underlined means indicate exits which had significantly different responses from starred means at .05 level of significance.
** Means calculated for categories 1.-5 (1=Very UnLikely; 2=Unlikely; 3=Neutral; 4=Likely; 5=Very Likely), category 0 (Don't Know) is omitted from calculation.
***Highlighted P-values indicate statistically significant differences at .05 level of significance.

Table 7.
Relationship Between Perceptions of Impacts from Tourism on the Blue Ridge Parkway and Attitudes toward Scenic Resource Protection Techniques*

| Technique Categories | Total Sample | Perceptions of Impacts Index Categories | | |
|---|---|---|---|---|
| | | Small Tourist Area | Small Urban Area | Large Urban Area |
| Land Acquisition | .1588 | -.0329 | .2545 | .4413 |
| Land Transfer Controls | .2587 | .0822 | .3055 | .4746 |
| Land Use Controls | .2627 | .2028 | .3289 | -.0716 |
| Land Development Controls | .3254 | .2419 | .4373 | .1932 |
| Tax Incentives | .3106 | .4776 | .1941 | -.0377 |
| Planning | .2356 | .1755 | .2644 | .2106 |
| Sign Controls | .1566 | .0261 | .2179 | .2078 |
| View Protection | .1481 | .0835 | .2517 | -.0191 |
| Voluntary Approaches | .0338 | -.0893 | .0855 | .1637 |

*Data presented as correlation coefficients

which rely on visual resources. Contradictions in policies related to the pursuit for preservation and desires for commercial development often occur in tourism zones. Several authors have contended that more potential lies in the enjoyment and preservation of rural lands, such as the those associated with the parkway, as attractions to tourists rather than in the development of the lands themselves (Cordell, McLellan, & Legg 1979; McNeely & Thorsell 1989; Forester, cited in Fagence 1990; Place 1991). The results from this study show that community leaders do feel that the parkway is important to their communities. In addition, protection of the visual resources associated with the parkway is also important to them. Although the majority of leaders indicated that the presence of the parkway has had limited effect on land use planning in the past, they indicated that scenic resource protection techniques are important tools that should be utilized by government officials to protect the parkway from incompatible development. The problem, however, lies in determining what types of controls will be accepted by different communities. It was determined in this study that probable acceptance of different techniques is not based on development level. However, they do suggest that landowners are more likely to accept techniques that are less restrictive and more voluntary in nature.

In considering strategies for tourism development along the parkway, we must consider what types of techniques will be accepted by private landowners along the parkway. The problem along the parkway is that the parkway itself controls very little land (Everhardt, cited in Elliott 1993). Several conservation groups and organizations are advocating better protection and control along the parkway. Unregulated development of this environment has the potential to change the resource base and affect the lives of local communities.

The development of policies is an important part of the planning process which recognizes the need for the husbandry of resources which support the tourism industry and contribute to local economies. The roles of controls and incentives are critical in managing tourism and its impacts (Travis 1982; Gunn 1988). Many alternative forms of tourism strive to conserve the natural resource, deepen the visitor experience, and enhance the social and economic well-being of the community. Sustainable development can only be attained through integrated resource management and land use planning (Tarnes & Hassan 1990). Mountain tourism should be organic and limited to growth that does not go beyond sustainable development.

Possible options to address development problems in western North Carolina have been identified as: regional based management, county based planning, case by case planning, and no state involvement (North Carolina Center for Public Policy Research 1990). Respondents to this study, in contrast, were most supportive of government intervention at the federal and state levels. In the United States and specifically on lands along the parkway, private property rights and land use priorities are sensitive and important issues. Strategies for sustainable development should include both the environment and the human element, and they must be integrated into national, regional, and community planning efforts (Cordell, McLellan, & Legg 1979; Cronin 1990). Past studies have recommended the adoption of holistic approaches to tourism development which balance economic concerns with social and environmental ones (Liu, Sheldon, & Var 1987; Choy 1991). Sadler (cited in Clark 1990) suggested that in order to link tourism development with consideration for the environment, supply side analysis and planning, as well as market intelligence is required. Tourism on the Blue Ridge Parkway is an environmentally dependent industry. Although some specific communities along the parkway have enacted land use regulations to protect the parkway, no comprehensive regional planning has taken place.

As previously mentioned, this study has shown that landowners along the parkway are more likely to accept techniques that are less restrictive and more voluntary in nature. In their efforts to work with local communities to develop planning strategies that will protect the parkway, the National Park Service should take these results into consideration. In addition, future research related to the perceptions and attitudes of the actual landowners is suggested. Although this would be a very large task, it would allow planners to more specifically determine the actual attitudes of landowners toward impacts of the parkway, tourism development, and scenic resource protection techniques.

Application of a marketing model, which utilizes a traditional marketing mix (product, price, place, and promotion), could be utilized by the National Park Service and other organizations interested in protecting the parkway from incompatible development. A strategy such as this could be used to educate and inform residents of the importance and benefits associated with maintaining the aesthetic quality of the parkway as a scenic resource. Using specific promotional tools, the parkway could be redefined in residents' minds as a product verses just a place. As a product, the parkway could be presented in conjunction with the intangible concepts of conservation and land use restrictions, instead of the more tangible elements associated with land development. The price component of the marketing mix could be used as a tool to portray the opportunity costs associated with conservation, balanced against the revenues associated with certain types of development. Furthermore, the idea that everyone benefits from conservation could be used in conjunction with this marketing concept. Identification of specific target markets such as private landowners, general residents, business owners, community leaders, and elected officials could then be used with a promotional strategy to effectively distribute these ideas and related information. Direct mail pieces, public service announcements, or informational programs on local cable networks, for example, could be used to reach residents and private landowners in their homes. In addition, a professional lobbyist could be used by some organizations to reach the legislative market. Furthermore, research data related to: economic impacts of travelers, environmental impacts associated with development, visual preferences of travelers, and perceptions of local residents, are very important to supporting preservation of the scenic integrity of the parkway.

## REFERENCES

Agresti, A., & B. Finlay. *Statistical Methods for the Social Sciences*, (2nd ed.). San Francisco, CA: Macmillan, 1986.

Ahmed, S. A. "Understanding Residents' Reaction to Tourism Marketing." *Journal of Travel Research 25*(2), 13-18, 1986.

Allen, L. R., P. T. Long, R. R. Perdue, & S. Kieselback. "The Impact of Tourism Development on Residents' Perceptions of Community Life." *Journal of Travel Research 27*(1), 16-21, 1988.

Belisle, F. J., & D. R. Hoy. "The Perceived Impact of Tourism by Residents: A Case Study in Santa Marta, Columbia." *Annals of Tourism Research 7*(1), 83-101, 1980.

Bergstrom, J. C., K. H. Cordell, A. F. Watson, & G. A. Ashley. "Economic Impacts of State Parks on State Economies in the South." *Southern Journal of Agricultural Economics 22*(2), 69-78, 1990.

*Blue Ridge Parkway: Establishment, Administration, and Maintenance*, 1936, § 460a-2, 16 U.S.C., 1988.

Choy, D. J. L. "The Case for 'Market Failure.'" *Tourism Management 12*(4), 313-330, 1991.

Clark, J. R. "Carrying Capacity: Defining the Limits to Coastal Tourism." In M. L. Miller & J. Auyong (Eds.), *Proceedings of the 1990 Congress on Coastal and Marine Tourism*, (pp. 118-131). Honolulu, Hawaii, USA: National Coastal Resources & Development Institute, 1990.

Computing Resource Center. *STATA Reference Manual*, (release 3, vol. 1-3, 5th ed.). Santa Monica, CA: Author, 1992.

Cordell, H. K., J. C. Bergstrom, & A. F. Watson. "Economic Growth and Interdependent Effects of State Park Visitation in Local and State Economies." *Journal of Leisure Research 24*, 253-268, 1992.

Cordell, H. K., R. W. McLellan, & M. H. Legg. "Managing Private Rural Land as a Visual Resource." In D. E. Hawkins, E. A. Shafer, & J. M. Rovelstad (Eds.), *Tourism Planning and Development Issues*, (pp. 87-97). Washington, DC: George Washington University, 1979.

Cronin, L. "A Strategy for Tourism and Sustainable Developments." *World Leisure and Recreation*, pp. 18-22, 1990.

Davis, C. "Developers, Park Service, Battle over Blue Ridge." *Sunday Journal and Sentinel*, p. unknown, 1970.

Davis, D., J. Allen, & R. M. Cosenza. "Segmenting Local Residents by Their Attitudes, Interests, and Opinions Toward Tourism." *Journal of Travel Research 27*(2), 2-8, 1988.

Dillman, D. A. *Mail and Telephone Surveys: The Total Design Method*. New York: John Wiley and Sons, 1978.

Duffield, B. S., & J. Long. "Tourism in the Highlands and Islands of Scotland: Rewards and Conflicts." *Annals of Tourism Research 8*(3), 403-431, 1981.

Elliott, F. "Unnatural Shadows Begin to Fall on the Blue Ridge Parkway." *The Winston-Salem Journal*, pp. A1, A8, 1993.

Fagence, M. "Geographically-Referenced Planning Strategies to Resolve Potential Conflict Between Environmental Values and Commercial Interests in Tourism Development in Environmentally Sensitive Areas." *Journal of Environmental Management 31*, 1-18, 1990.

Farrell, B. "Tourism's Human Conflicts: Cases from the Pacific." *Annals of Tourism Research 6*(2), 122-136, 1979.

Fridgen, J. D. *Dimensions of Tourism*. East Lansing, Michigan: Educational Institute of the American Hotel & Motel Association, 1991.

Futrell, J. W. "NEPA and the Parks: Use it or Lose it." In D. J. Simon (Ed.), *Our Common Lands, Defending the National Parks*, (pp. 107-126).

Washington, DC, Covelo, CA: Island Press, 1988.

Gunn, C. E. *Tourism Planning.* New York: Taylor and Francis, 1988.

Hastings, S. E., & S. M. Brucker. *An Introduction to Regional Input-Output Analysis.* Paper Prepared for Conference on Input-Output Modeling and Economic Development Applications, Kansas City, MO, 1989.

Holmes, B. F. "On Blending Tourism with Natural Beauty." In D. E. Hawkins, E. A. Shafer, & J. M. Rovelstad (Eds.), *Tourism Planning and Development Issues*, (pp. 90-106). Washington, DC: George Washington University, 1979.

Keiter, R. "National Park Protection: Putting the Organic Act to Work." In D. J. Simon (Ed.), *Our Common Lands, Defending the National Parks*, (pp. 75-87). Washington, DC, Covelo, CA: Island Press, 1988.

Knopp, T. B. "Tourism, the Local Interest and The Function of Public Lands." In D. E. Hawkins, E. A. Shafer, & J. M. Rovelstad (Eds.), *Tourism Planning and Development Issues*, (pp. 225-237). Washington, DC: George Washington University, 1979.

Liu, J. C., P. T. Sheldon, & T. Var. "Resident Perceptions of the Environmental Impacts of Tourism." *Annals of Tourism Research 14*,17-37, 1978.

Liu, J. C., & T. Var. Resident attitudes toward tourism impacts in Hawaii. *Annals of Tourism Research 13*,193-214, 1986.

Long, P. T., R. R. Perdue, & L. Allen. Rural resident tourism perceptions and attitudes by community level of tourism. *Journal of Travel Research 28*(3), 3-9, 1990.

Makowski, E. H. *Scenic Parks and Landscape Values.* New York, London: Garland Publishing, Inc., 1990.

McNeely, J. A., & J. W. Thorsell. "Jungles, Mountains, and Islands: How Tourism Can Help Conserve the Natural Heritage." *World Leisure and Recreation 31*(4), 29-39, 1989.

Mountain Ridge Protection Act of 1983, §113A-205, 14, N.C. Code .

Murphy, P. E. "Community Attitudes to Tourism: A Comparative Analysis." *International Journal of Tourism Management 2*(3),189-195, 1981.

Murphy, P. E. "Perceptions and Attitudes of Decision-Making Groups in Tourism Centers." *Journal of Travel Research 21*(3), 8-12, 1983.

North Carolina Center for Public Policy Research. *Promises in the Promised Land* (video). Chapel Hill, NC: North Carolina Public Television, 1990.

Pizam, A. "Tourism's Impacts: The Social Costs to the Destination Community as Perceived by its Residents." *Journal of Travel Research 16*(4), 8-12, 1978.

Place, S. E. Nature tourism and rural development in Tortuguero. *Annals of Tourism Research 18*, 186-201, 1991.

Ross, G. F. "Resident Perceptions of the Impact of Tourism on an Australian City." *Journal of Travel Research 30*(3), 13-17, 1992.

Rothman, R. A. "Resident and Transients: Community Reaction to Seasonal Visitors." *Journal of Travel Research 16*(3), 8-13, 1978.

Runya, D., & C. Wu. "Assessing Tourism's More Complex Consequences." *Annals of Tourism Research 6*, 448-463, 1979.

Scenic America. *Press Release: Scenic America to Recognize America's 20 Most Important Scenic Byways.* Available from: Mary Ann Lasch, Scenic America, 21 Dupont Circle, Washington, DC 20036, 1992.

Sethna, R. J. "Social Impact of Tourism in Selected Caribbean Countries." In D. E. Hawkins, E. A. Shafer, & J. M. Rovelstad (Eds.), *Tourism Planning and Development Issues*, (pp. 239-249). Washington, DC: George Washington University, 1979.

Sheldon, P. J., & T. Var. "Resident Attitudes to Tourism in North Wales." *Tourism Management 5*(1), 40-47, 1984.

Sommer, R., & B. B. Sommer. *A Practical Guide to Behavioral Research.* New York: Oxford University Press, 1980.

Southeastern Research Institute. *Final Case Study for the National Scenic Byways Study: A Case Study for the Blue Ridge Parkway.* (Publication No. FHWA-ED 90-043). Atlanta: U.S. Department of Transportation, Federal Highway Administration, 1990.

Stynes, D. E. *Visitor Spending and the Local Economy: Great Smoky Mountains National Park.* Unpublished manuscript, 1992.

Swanson, E. W. *Travel and the National Parks: An Economic Study.* Washington, DC: Dept. of the Interior, National Park Service, 1969.

Tarnes, D. A., & K. Hassan. "Sustainable Development in Marine Tourism for South Johar Malaysia: The Aseansuaid Coastal Resources Management Project." In M. L. Miller & J. Auyong (Eds.), *Proceedings of the 1990 Congress on Coastal and Marine Tourism*, (pp. 93-99). Honolulu: National Coastal Resources & Development Institute, 1990.

Thomason, P., J. L. Crompton, & B. D. Kamp. "A Study of the Attitudes of Impacted Groups within a Host Community Toward Prolonged Stay Tourist Visitors." *Journal of Travel Research* *17*(3), 2-6, 1979.

Travis, A. S. "Managing the Environmental and Cultural Impacts of Tourism and Leisure Development." *Tourism Management 3*(4), 256-262, 1982.

United States Travel Data Center. *The Economic Impact of U.S. Travel on North Carolina Counties*. Washington, DC: Author, 1992.

Williams, D. Personal Interview regarding current research efforts in Virginia, 1992.

Williams, R. A. *The Regional Impact of The Blue Ridge Parkway in Virginia*. Blacksburg, VA: Virginia Polytechnic Institute and State University, 1981.

Williams, R. A., & C. R. Knoeber. *Economic Impacts of the Blue Ridge Parkway in Virginia and North Carolina*. Blacksburg, VA: Virginia Polytechnic Institute and State University, 1979.

# Landscape Visibility Studies for a U.S. Forest Service Scenic Byway: Mount Rogers National Recreation Area, Virginia

*William E. Shepherd and Lynn Crafts*

## Context for Landscape Visibility Studies Along Roadway Corridors

Over the last 30 years or so, automobile touring has continued to be one of the top two forms of outdoor recreation, walking being the other. With the continued and expanded use of transportation corridors for recreation and tourism, there has been a dramatic increase in the concern and interest shown for scenic roadways. These roadways fall predominately into four (4) categories: scenic byways, parkways, scenic roads and interstate highways. The focus of this work is on the scenic byways which have experienced the most dramatic changes in use and development pressures over the last several years. This change is due to a shift from established roads which provide local automobile and service access to more remote areas to a roadway that provides access to cultural, recreational and economical facilities. The access distinguishes scenic byways from other scenic roadways. The difference is that they are generally identified and designated existing improved rural roadways within the state highway system. This means that the view areas are most often not developed in association with the roadway, but are a product of the context in which the road is located. Scenic byway designation highlights the roadways importance and increase the diversity of users beyond the local automobile and service traffic to include all forms of recreation vehicles, such as bikes and motorcycles. With the completion of most of the federal interstate highway program and the recently passed Internodal Surface Transportation Efficiency Act (ISTEA), the importance of scenic byways has come to the forefront of planning and management concerns in the United States.

Scenic byways and other corridors, like parkways, greenways, trails and rivers, are a major component to maintaining public access to many of the natural and cultural amenities of our country. Scenic byways are defined by the Federal Highway Administration as " road(s) having roadsides or corridors of high natural beauty and cultural or historic value" (U.S.D.O.T., 1988, p. 1-1) As scenic corridors are identified and promoted for attracting tourists and developers, for presenting the cultural and environmental diversity of America, for taking the pressure off of highways and connecting or reconnecting people with the land, they are changing from a way to get to somewhere else to a destination in and of themselves. How scenic corridors are planned, designed, designated and managed is critical to achieving these ends. The pressures of development, increased traffic flow and changing land use patterns all jeopardize the original character of designated corridors.

There are many public and private entities that see the importance of careful planning and managing of these corridors.

---

Note: This presentation is dedicated to Dr. William E. Shepherd who passed away after developing this work and before the completion of the research for this project. I am indebted to him for his work on this project.

Giving them a variety of tools with which to do inventories and analyze the qualities of the areas will insure quality plans that can be implemented and supported by the citizens of the area.

## Approach to Landscape Visibility Studies

In order to more fully understand the characteristics of a particular corridor, and to help insure that appropriate management techniques are implemented, visual studies can be applied. Development of a visual assessment approach that looks predominately at visibility in the landscape is a process that accomplishes this end. Visibility (as the term is used in visual assessment studies) describes an area or areas that can be seen and understood from a particular point or path in the landscape. (Smardon et al., 1986)

A compilation of the studies has developed four specific visibility procedures which provide for a greater understanding of the landscape. These procedures are used as tools to demonstrate what is important or significant along the study corridor. The procedures also determine how understanding of the landscape through resource management can be accomplished. The set of tools was composed of the following procedures:

- defining and mapping the extent of the scenic corridor
- determining and diagraming distance zones
- mapping visibility, including frequency and magnitude of views
- preparing an analysis of the corridor envelope.

The studies were conducted in response to the need for greater understanding of the landscape, a refinement of visibility studies, development of a set of tools to be used for visual analysis and development of better corridor management techniques. Most of the studies were performed for the Mount Rogers Scenic Byway in southwestern Virginia. The byway, within the USFS Jefferson National Forest, is part of the major access and circulation link through the Recreation Area. The research, which was primarily developed in the field, built upon, followed and refined techniques developed and presented by Dr. William E. Shepherd for the Third Biennial Linear Parks Conference in 1989. It also relied heavily on the research of Burt Litton for the United States Forest Service (USFS) (1968, 1973) and Donald Appleyard (Appleyard, Lynch & Myer, 1966) and Kevin Lynch (1960) in the 1960s and 1970s.

The visibility studies developed were used as analytical tools to inventory, interpret and manage the visual resources of scenic corridors. Combining the results of these studies helped to determine existing patterns of the land, management practices, the deficiencies in these practices and an understanding for future directions of the byway's management.

## Study Area

The primary site for developing these procedures was Mount Rogers Scenic Byway, in southwest Virginia. The USFS requested that we develop an interpretive management plan for the Mount Rogers Scenic Byway which goes through Mount Rogers National Recreation Area (NRA). The results of this research on landscape visibility were used in the development of the Mount Rogers interpretive management plan.

The area of the byway is in between the physiographic provinces of the Ridge and Valley and the Blue Ridge. The focus of this study is the 23 miles section of the byway within the NRA, between the small towns of Troutdale and Damascus. The byway corridor runs through an upland valley with rolling hills and flat valley bottoms and down a rocky gorge. It is flanked by open fields, some agriculture, settlements, and young mixed deciduous forests. Views along the road are limited and constrained with occasional larger views. The larger views are primarily of Iron Mountain to the north and the shoulders of Mount Rogers to the south, with occasional views of the crest and nearby mountain tops.

## Recommendations

The research conducted provides some very clear understandings about the use of visual analysis for better presenting, maintaining and managing scenic corridors. The recommendations for management and interpretation were derived from the results of studies conducted along the Mount Rogers Scenic Byway. The recommendations included:

- development of glens along the byway, which reflect the character and development patterns of the area
- provide views of specific ridges that enhance an understanding of where one is located in the landscape (i.e., visual boundaries and focal points)
- close views to areas that do not provide an understanding of the area (i.e., screening views that compromise the visual values established for the area)
- expand view opportunities of the entire landscapes (i.e., long and distant views), which may be snap shots for the area
- add trees along fence existing or abandoned rows to define cultural influences, to frame open pasture views and to enhance real or symbolic landscape patterns
- develop a series of visual 'events', or specialized sequence, that reflect the character of the byway experience (i.e., views of the fields from midslope that close down to forest tunnels with glens that appear before intersecting or entry roads)

During this process several basic problems arose which created a difficulty in understanding the landscape. Maintaining and enhancing the many of the natural and cultural attributes of scenic corridors, such as those that touch the senses, were the primary role of the management plan. It is critical that managers and designers understand the landscape they are working in so that they can enhance and preserve the attributes that make each scenic byway corridor unique.

## Study Procedures

Recommendations derived from this analysis are predicated on a clear definition of the intent and goals of the designation of the scenic byway or corridor. These procedures were used in conjunction with other typical land analysis studies, including; land ownership, land use, site analysis, and so on. Primarily, the procedures presented here are set of tools that can be used to get a clear understanding (from a visual perspective) of the character, patterns and uniqueness of a particular scenic corridor. This information is most helpful for preserving, protecting and maintaining those qualities.

## Defining and Mapping the Scenic Corridor

The first procedure is defining and mapping the scenic corridor. The scenic corridor is "the visible land area outside the highway right-of-way" (Smardon et al., 1986, p. 313). The intent of this step is to ascertain the extent of area to be examined for the project and to understand the corridor as a whole. Initial mapping is done in the office with USGS quad sheets by highlighting the road and then outlining the potential visible area from the road, primarily along the ridge tops adjacent to the road, which often corresponds to watershed divides. The limits of the scenic corridor are the edges of all those areas that may be seen from the road. Military crests greatly influence and reduce the breadth of the scenic corridor. However, these are more difficult to identify, so office mapping will usually be from ridge line to ridge line.[1] Generally, the overall area mapped is greater than what is actually seen. Follow up must be made with cross sections, field verification and mapping to have a more accurate corridor delineation, as called for by the particular project.

In the field what will be found are distinct patches, or small areas, seen from given points, the composite of these is called the viewshed. Irregularities in the viewshed edge and areas are due to the landform and vegetative cover which limit and direct areas that are seen within the corridor. A compilation of these patches will give a much greater area and a clear understanding of what is seen.

For the Mount Rogers Scenic Byway we found that the north side of the corridor had a clear edge following Iron Mountain Ridge (on the ridge and valley province side of the byway). However, on the south side, which was in the Blue Ridge province, the visual edge was harder to discern and required more field and cross-sectional work.

## Defining and Diagraming Distance Zones

Before beginning the second procedure, which is defining and diagraming distance zones, a determination of how the data will be collected must be completed. Information is best collected photographically in the field and then taken to the office for analysis. There are several ways of determining what is photographed.

The selection of either predetermined points or continuous data collection is critical for insuring a clear understanding of the possibilities and limitations offered by the data collected. The following are descriptions of four approaches that could be used. Depending on the type and extent of information being collected, selection of the appropriate approach is important and has its own set of strengths and weaknesses.

The first selection approach is the designation of a standard distance or *station points (SP)* along the road (Figure 1). The advantages of this approach is that it is an equal distribution of information gathered along the corridor making it simpler to determine and diagram by reducing the amount of information that needs to be analyzed.

Figure 1.

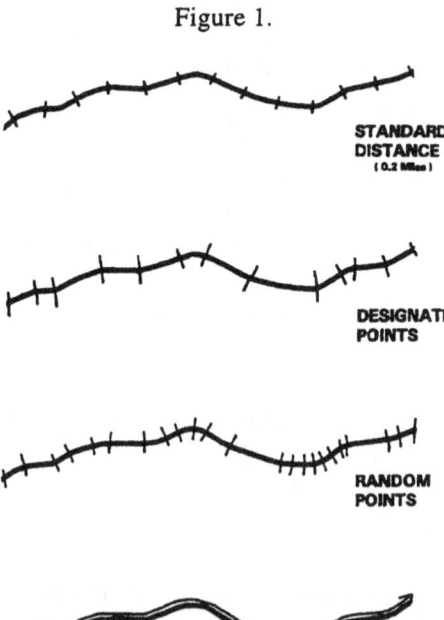

STANDARD DISTANCE (0.2 Miles)

DESIGNATED POINTS

RANDOM POINTS

CONTINUOUS MAPPING

The disadvantages are that there may be important information lost between the points and that a lot of information may be collected that is not essential to the study objectives. This selection approach is used for the majority of the research along the Mount Rogers Scenic Byway with a designated distance of 0.2 of a mile.

The second selection approach is the designation of *critical points* along the roadway. The advantage here is that important points can be determined and thoroughly studied. Points are determined by proximity to important views, facilities or features; by safety concerns; or other criteria established by the project goals and objectives. This approach also limits unnecessary field work (Figure 1). The disadvantages are that in selecting points early in the process it may not be evident as to which points will provide the necessary information. Furthermore, after critical point selection there may be other areas or points that may also be critical to obtaining a thorough understanding of the corridor. Re-selection later in the process is possible, although this may require additional field work. The critical point technique was used on the corridor envelope analysis portion of our studies and for critical view areas that were not covered by our use of standard distances or station point.

Choosing *random points* along the road is the third possible selection approach. The problems with this method seem to far outweigh its general applicability to visibility work (Figure 1). Problems include: the inability to identify all important features; a poor understanding of patterns, especially in linear or sequential corridors; and difficulty in mapping and understanding the corridor. After experimenting with this procedure we found that it was not acceptable for gathering reliable information along the byway.

The final selection approach, *continuous mapping* seems the most logical as since all parts of the roadway and vistas are included (Figure 1). How areas relate to each other is readily visible and any alterations required along the corridor could be easily understood in context. The problem with this approach has to do with recording. A video tape provides the most complete record of the corridor. It also allows for a sense of the speed by which the corridor can or will be driven as well as an understanding of what can be seen when driving at a particular speed. However, mapping all the information is time consuming and difficult and may mean the recording of a lot of unnecessary information. Another fact that is worthy of consideration is a statement by the American Society of Civil Engineers Practical Highway Esthetics report of 1977 which stated:

> At even moderate speeds it takes about 1/16 second for the eye to fixate on an object so it can be perceive. The eye always jumps from one point of fixation to the next, and it sees absolutely nothing between jumps. . . . This fact implies that continuous recording may not even be accurate, in terms of how the visitor perceives the corridor, therefore making it unnecessary. (Cron, 1977, p. 14)

Once the most appropriate technique for collecting information has been selected, the analysis of the distance zones can begin. The purpose of this step is to look at the continuity or discontinuity of the views, the sequence of views and distance zones, and the proportional relationships of the distance zones. Distance zones encompass all the areas seen from a given point. They are divided into three (3) primary distance groupings based on the clarity and complexity of the landscape to reduce the complexity of the analysis

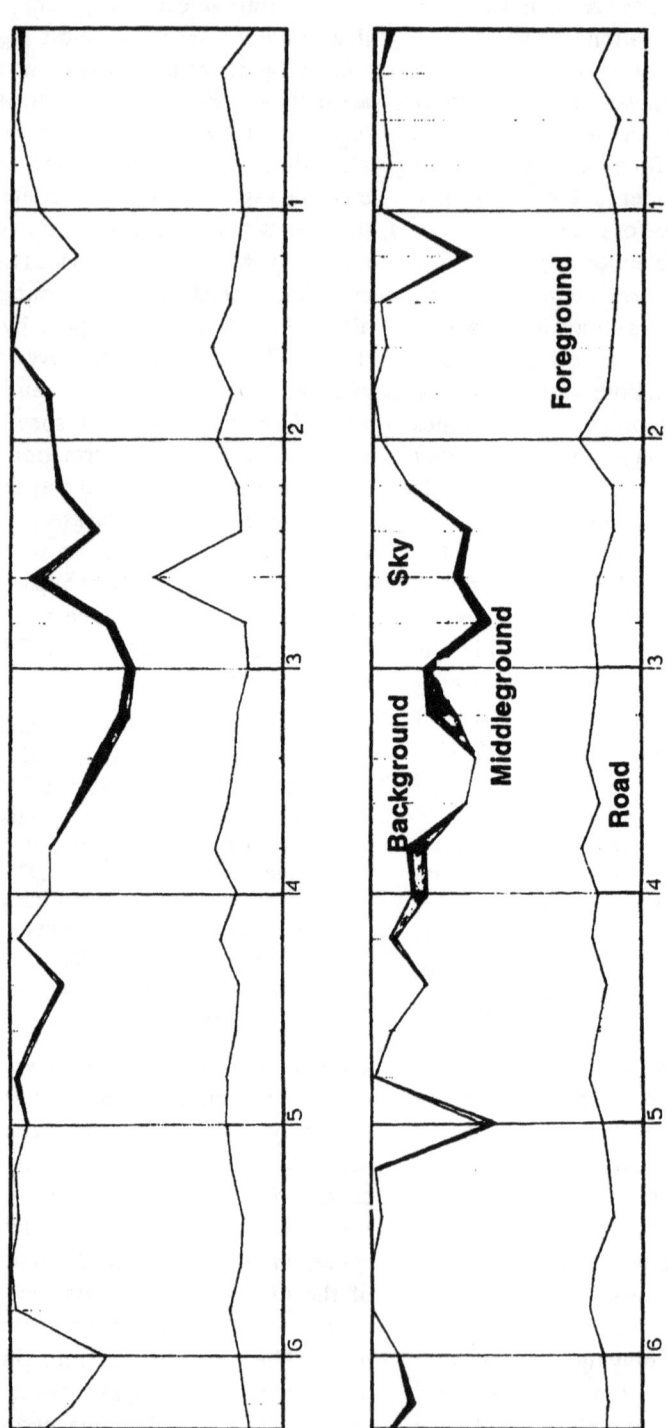

Figure 2. Distance Zones.
Growing Season SP 0.0 to 6.0

(Smardon et al., 1986). These distance zones are: foreground, middleground and background. These designations follow Litton's work, modified for the Appalachian landscape, which is less distinct and has more distance restrictions due to atmospheric conditions and a more generally rolling topography.

The foreground is that area where details and minute textures can be seen, where colors are bright and varied and where human scale is comprehendible. Middleground encompasses the area where entire features can be seen, textures are still noticeable and colors start to blend. The distant background is the skyline area, the frame or backdrop which allows the other zones to be more clearly understood. Colors of the background in the Appalachian region are predominately shades of blue and the textures of the background are mostly nonexistent and are very dependent on the weather.

Along the Mount Rogers Scenic Byway at the designated road speeds, approximately 35 m.p.h., it was later proven that the distance zones had the following ranges:

foreground ....... 0.0 to 0.2 miles

middleground .... 0.2 to 1.0 miles

background ...... 1.0 to 5.0 miles

The study of the Appalachian landscape reveals its many subtle and complex characteristics. Through studying the complexity of the Appalachian landscape, it is realized that the Appalachian landscape has many subtle characteristics. In the study area foreground views are made up of two designations: the first is up to 0.2 of a mile distance from the road and the other is the '*intimate foreground*' which actually created a physical response in the traveler. The responses created are those that use the senses: the smell of the flowers and trees along the road, the feel of the humidity or coolness next to a stream, the sound of the birds or wind. Many of these responses are lost to the traveler who moves at speeds greater than about 25-35 miles an hour or who drives on a road corridor where the road does not reflect the land.

Station point slides are the best way to record the distance zones. This procedure is best accomplished by driving the corridor and taking slides in both directions at each station point. Whether or not side photographs are taken will depend on the amount of information necessary to accomplish the objectives of the project. Ideally the slides should be taken in the growing and dormant season to get a clear understanding of the existing corridor and the potentials for views and understanding which can only be experienced when the leaves are down.

The slides are to be taken back to the office, projected on a grid and percentages of foreground, middleground, background, sky and road totaled. Totals are then tallied, put on a graph and colored to show the arrangement of distant and narrow views and an understanding of the overall visual sequence (Figure 2).

**Mapping Visibility**

The next step is to map these view zones to create an understanding of the total land area involved, its magnitude, how often an area is seen, its frequency, and where an area is seen from. This procedure is done by looking at the photos and mapping visible areas. Mapping visibility, as with data collection, is done in both the growing and dormant seasons while driving in both directions along the corridor, for a total of four maps. Mapping the middleground and background areas is most critical as these are the zones that orient the traveler to the landscape. These zones are usually seen from several places, several distances and for longer periods of time.

The visible areas are delineated and than a line is drawn connecting the delineated areas to the station points from which they were photographed. These lines give an indication of the number of station points that have similar views and from where areas that need to be managed are seen. This also identifies the areas with the most continuous views, those that last the longest while moving along the corridor.

When all station points are mapped review of the results will give a sense of how much area may need to be managed. With this information views can be opened or screened depending on the resources and project objectives. This process established that in the Appalachian landscape middleground generally starts around 0.2 of a mile and background (depending on the weather) around 0.75 to 1 mile. Determination of these distances came from measuring the distances from the station points to the areas of middle ground and background that were mapped.

Frequency is the number of times a particular part of the landscape is seen from various points along the corridor. This is particularly important as it relates to the continuous mapping, as many sites may be seen from sites between selected points. Once the sites are mapped, their size can be calculated. The amounts of area seen can be tallied and graphed to determine the magnitude of the view. For example: at SP #4 two (2) square miles of middleground view are visible; at SP #5 only 0.75 sq. mi. of middleground are visible; therefore SP #4 has a higher magnitude, even though it views fewer areas than SP #5. The graph will give an idea of the complexity of the landscape. It will reflect how large the areas are that need to be considered for management and how many separate land areas are involved. Then, it is up to the management to determine which areas are most important to be managed, either to actively or through a hands off approach.

## Preparing an Analysis of the Corridor Envelope

The final step is the preparation and analysis of the *corridor envelope*. The corridor envelope is the three dimensional area surrounding the road. More specifically, the entire cross-section of the road corridor at any given point, including the road plane and everything above it. This procedure has two phases. The first phase consists of analyzing the overall corridor visual experience and is effected at a larger scale than the second phase.

Phase one is used to show areas along the road with similar characteristics as well as areas seen from the road. These studies were performed driving in both directions along the road and were primarily fashioned after Burt Litton's research on landscape descriptions (1968). The results of this study can be used to understand the patterns of experiences and the uniqueness of sections of the byway.

The second phase consists of analyzing the corridor experience as it relates to the land, while focusing on the foreground experience. Phase two includes a detailed look at the components next to the road, the features adjacent to the road and the intimate foreground experience. Components of this phase primarily had to do with the smaller envelope of the floor (or road surface and platform) and the walls and ceiling (or what is along and over the road). Information was recorded on the road alignment, the situation of the road (including the place in the landscape where the viewer is located), viewer position, road surface characteristics, the compositional aspects of the road (including roadside vegetation placement and

Figure 3. Road Grade

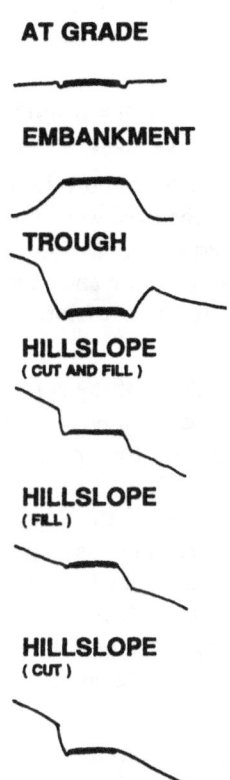

makeup), where the viewer is looking, what the view characteristics are and miscellaneous features. All of these components will help define and determine roadside management. (See Figures 3-7 for diagrams of road alignment and road situation characteristics.)

Both phases of corridor envelope analysis help define: corridor visibility, foreground complexity, viewer position, and sequence of experience. The results can influence and guide the design of the aspects of visibility, complexity and sequence as well as the management of the roadway, the right-of-way and adjacent foreground areas.

## Discussion

Analysis of these four procedures (defining and mapping the scenic corridor, defining and diagraming distance zones, mapping visibility, and preparing the analysis of the corridor envelope) facilitates three processes: recognition and understanding of how land patterns are laid out, what order the land is viewed in (sequence) and how many variables there are for the scenic corridor. At a time when scenic byways are forced into the forefront due to their tourism and development attributes, preservation of the quality of the corridor is imperative. The tools presented here provide for an analysis of the opportunities and limitations of the corridor, as well as, identifying the areas that are hard to comprehend or are poorly defined. An area that is hard to comprehend is one that has too many elements in one view. Through design and management, accentuation of more pleasant areas and screening of less desirable areas can be accomplished. With the areas of concern identified, site specific recommendations can be made which will guide the future management and development of the area.

Figure 4. Compositional Feature / Position

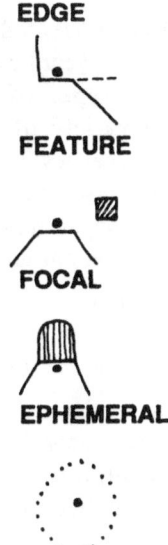

Figure 5. Compositional Wall

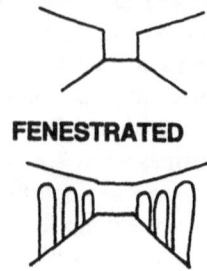

Recommendations include suggestions for plantings, clearings, mowing schedules, fencing and other appropriate management practices. Areas are be identified for planting to enhance or focus particular views or cover up others. Specific recommendations for the purchase or designation of view easements can be enacted to locate, control or restrict development. A very important aspect of this analysis is that the inherent character of the landscape surrounding the byway can be identified so that adequate maintenance and enhancement of the character of the byway will occur. This maintenance will insure continued use and prevention of degradation of the corridor.

The research presented here was conducted over a two year time period. It included various types of recording techniques in a variety of situations, including seasonal changes. The thoroughness of the process insured a clear understanding that in the Appalachian landscape the following observations are reliable:

- scenic corridors are simple to determine in the ridge and valley province through following the ridge lines
- station points are the most reliable and comprehensive recording of information, especially if augmented by site specific data collection at critical points
- distance zones are variable, depending on the season and weather, and far shorter than western landscapes
- mapping of visibility is important to determining the location and extent of resource management
- analysis of the corridor envelope is a comprehensive way of understanding the sequence, rhythm and character of the corridor and identifying possible location of intervention practices.

Further analysis of the corridor envelope procedure needs to be done before it will be a vital tool for choreographing the corridor experience. It is imperative that the experience of the corridor becomes better understood as more and more 'riders' of all types use scenic corridors frequently. For the character and uniqueness of each one is the drawing card which needs to be protected and enhanced, to

Figure 6. Compositional Landform

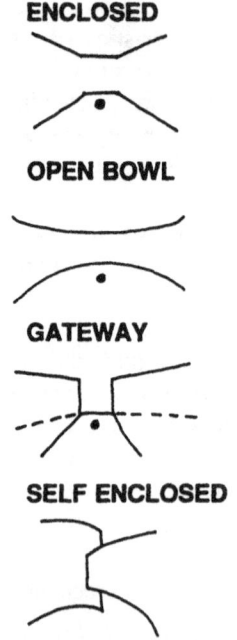

Figure 7. Compositional Ceiling

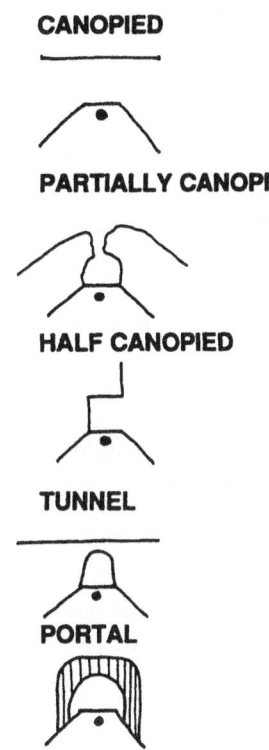

offset and deter the pressures inherent in their attractiveness.

## Conclusion

In order for scenic corridors throughout the United States to continue to be places that are pleasant and interesting to go to and to keep them as a resource to be protected, studies like these that set up a strong framework for decision making to be done to insure the character of the corridors. These visibility studies (scenic corridor boundaries identification, scenic zone designation, visibility diagrams of frequency and magnitude and analysis of the corridor envelope) are useful tools for understanding the character, weaknesses and potentials of the scenic corridor. The foundations that are based on informed decisions are critical for setting priorities for the maintenance or enhancement of existing conditions and character of the corridors. Whether the corridors are byways, country roads, trails, bike paths, river or streams, each needs to have visionary tools cultivated for them that carry out future preservation, development and management plans.

## REFERENCES

Appleyard, D., K. Lynch, and J. R. Myer. 1966. *The View from the Road.* Massachusetts Institute of Technology, Cambridge, MA.

Cron, F. W. 1977. *Practical Highway Aesthetics.* The Committee on Geometrics and Esthetics of Local Highway Division. American Society of Civil Engineers, New York.

Litton, R. B., Jr. 1968. *Forest Landscape Description and Inventories—A Basis for Land Planning and Design.* U.S. For. Service Research Paper PSW-49. Pacific S.W. For. and Range Exp. Stn., Berkeley, CA.

_____. 1973. *Landscape Control Points: A Procedure for Predicting and Monitoring Visual Impacts.* U.S.D.A. Research Paper PSW-91. Pacific S.W. For. and Range Exp. Stn., Berkeley, CA.

Lynch, K. 1960. *The Image of the City.* M.I.T. Press, Cambridge, MA.

Shepherd, W. E. 1989. "Visibility Description, Visual Analysis, and Land Use Control along Scenic Byways: A Case Study in Appalachian Mountains of Virginia and West Virginia." In *Parkways, Greenways, Riverways: The Way More Beautiful; Proceedings of the Third Biennial International Linear Parks Conference.* Appalachian Consortium Press, Boone, NC.

Smardon, R. C., J. F. Palmer, and J. P. Felleman, eds. 1986. *Foundations for visual project analysis.* John Wiley and Sons, New York.

U.S.D.O.T., Federal Highway Administration. 1988. *Scenic Byways.* U.S.D.O.T., F.H.W.A., Publication No. FHWA-DF-88-004, Washington, DC.

## NOTES

1. Military crests, often called military ridges, are those shoulders that interrupt the view of the crest from a given location. Military operations were often located on military crests since the enemy had a more difficult time seeing the them in that location.

# Protection of Scenic Resources Beyond Park Boundaries: A Case Study from Roanoke County, Virginia

*Janet Scheid*

## Background

The County of Roanoke is located in southwest Virginia and is the largest metropolitan area in this part of the State. The County is about 250 square miles in size and has a population of approximately 79,000. Virginia is one of the only states in the nation that still has independent cities so the City of Roanoke is not included in this population figure for the County. The City adds another 100,000 people and the entire metropolitan area is about 250,000 strong.

The Blue Ridge Parkway travels for nearly 470 miles through two states, 29 counties, three national forests and an Indian reservation. The Parkway descends from the Peaks of Otter and for nearly 27 miles travels through Roanoke County. Roanoke has the distinction of being the most urban, metropolitan stop along this scenic motor route.

## Roanoke County Zoning Ordinance

In 1986, the County began to revise and rewrite its twenty year old zoning ordinance. As part of this process the County proposed a comprehensive rezoning of all the land in the unincorporated parts of the County—approximately 44,000 parcels of property.

This revamping of the zoning ordinance was near completion 6 years later. In December 1992 the Roanoke County Planning Commission recommended rezoning hundreds of acres near the Blue Ridge Parkway, some with frontage on the Parkway, from an agricultural zoning district to a residential zoning district.

After input from the National Park Service—Blue Ridge Parkway Office, the County Board of Supervisors rezoned these properties to an agricultural zoning district "temporarily". The Board wanted more time to examine the impact of residential zoning on sensitive Parkway viewsheds and so set up a committee to study this issue.

## Viewshed Committee

The Viewshed Committee was formed in January 1993. The purpose of the Committee was to identify important viewsheds along the Parkway. The members of the committee were appointed by the County Administrator and consisted of two developers (one with financial interest in property along the Parkway), two National Park Service employees, one member of the Friends of the Blue Ridge Parkway, one Planning Commission member, and myself—a land use planner on the County's planning staff.

We began our study by defining the term "critical viewshed" and identifying these viewsheds in the County. As it meanders down the Blue Ridge Mountains, the Blue Ridge Parkway, America's first rural parkway provides the visitor with a leisurely trip through many diverse and beautiful environments. In Roanoke County this is probably more true than in a lot of other places on the Parkway. As I mentioned earlier, Roanoke is the most urban, metropolitan point along the Parkway. The Parkway, therefore provides a wonderful respite from the encroaching suburban development—houses, office buildings and shopping centers. The Parkway has been quite successful in providing visitors with the impression that they are in a park with boundaries that extend to the horizon.

In fact, this is not the case and this illusion is becoming more and more difficult to perpetuate in growing, urbanizing areas like Roanoke County, Virginia.

It is neither practical nor possible for the National Park Service to control all lands visible from the Parkway. As this rural parkway travels through a growing metropolitan area how do we preserve the cultural landscapes and scenic resources that are critical to the uniqueness of the Parkway? And who does the responsibility for this lie with? What about private property rights and the need for a growing community to provide housing to meet an ever increasing demand?

As our committee went to work these were some of the issues that were foremost in our minds.

## Results of the Committee's Work

We began by agreeing on some definitions. We agreed that a viewshed is a landscape that can be directly seen from the BRP.

We also came to a consensus on the factors that would determine whether an area was a critical viewshed. These factors are:

1. *Distance and visibility from the Parkway*—Critical viewsheds are generally in the foreground (quarter mile) of the area you can see. If there is a significant increase or decrease in elevation/topography or the existence of trees *on Parkway property* that shield an area from view, than that area is not a critical viewshed.

2. *Design*—The Parkway is a "planned design". Those areas that are planned and designed to attract the eye are critical viewsheds. This would include not only the scenic overlooks along the Parkway but also the designed vistas.

In order to maximize scenic views, the Parkway was located in terrain that normal roads would have avoided.

At the time construction on the Parkway began in 1935, there was little or no precedent for the building of a scenic road of this magnitude. Today the Parkway is recognized throughout the world as a significant engineering achievement.

3. *Development*—Critical viewsheds are pristine areas and can incur only minimum levels of change before destroying the character of that view. If development occurs in these areas it should enhance the rural character of the Park.

With these definitions as a starting point, we began our field work in February —the perfect time to assess views without being encumbered by tree foliage. We quickly found out that it was much easier to define "viewshed" and define "critical" on paper in an abstract sense than to go out in the field and apply these definitions.

We started with Geographic Information System maps depicting the portion of the Parkway in the County. These maps showed every parcel of property within 10,000 feet of the Parkway. We also studied and evaluated the USGS topographical maps of this area.

After many hours on the Parkway, working individually and as a group, we arrived at a consensus of where the critical viewsheds are in Roanoke County. We identified 11 critical viewshed areas. These viewsheds involved over one hundred parcels of property and over 500 acres of private land.

## Committee Recommendations

Our committee has made several recommendations:

1. The eleven critical viewsheds are important to the Parkway and the County and should be "protected".
2. The viewsheds should be down-zoned to the lowest density allowable under the Roanoke County Zoning Ordinance.
3. An overlay district should be designed for these viewsheds that would impose additional development standards for these areas.

Recommendation #3 merits further explanation and necessitates some discussion of Virginia planning legislation. This legislation conveys zoning authority from the State to the local governments and determines what can and cannot be regulated. Virginia is a Dillon Rule state. In the Commonwealth of Virginia, zoning is a legislative power vested in the State and delegated to the local governments. As a Dillon Rule state, local governments in Virginia only have the authority to do those things specifically spelled out in the Code of Virginia. In most other states, local governments can do anything not specifically prohibited by the State Code—this provides much more flexibility and the opportunity for creative solutions. The Code of Virginia states that local governments can regulate the use of property, the size and area of parcels, and the location, bulk, and height of structures. The County of Roanoke does not have the authority to regulate or impose design standards. For example, the County can not impose standards that regulate house paint colors, exterior materials, pitch of roof, or any other architectural standards.

The local government can impose development standards, as our committee has recommended. These may include such things as increased setbacks from the Parkway, height restrictions, increased landscaping requirements and fence standards.

## Perspectives of a Staff Planner

Roanoke County is a forward thinking and somewhat enlightened community. The administrative and legislative bodies in the County, as well as the general public, have an appreciation for the scenic beauty and economic benefits of the Blue Ridge Parkway. Granted we are not Eugene, Oregon or Boulder, Colorado but we have had zoning in some form for almost fifty years.

It is eminently clear to me that zoning is not enough, and in some cases may be detrimental to creative, environmentally sensitive design strategies. The County was ill prepared to deal with the issue of protecting Parkway viewsheds on private lands. The County does not have any type of conservation overlay district and no means of effectively denying a property owner the right to develop his or her property at some residential density level. There are no mandatory cluster development or open space provisions. Roanoke County has no greenway plan and no ridge top development restrictions. In short, having a County Zoning Ordinance and a County Comprehensive Plan are not enough. It is a start for sure, but the mechanisms must also be in place that allow us to identify, analyze, and than proceed to protect in an efficient, effective and legal manner those natural resources that the County deems critical.

The legislative body of any local government is by nature a political body. Politicians respond to pressure. In the case of the Roanoke County viewshed study, pressure has been brought to bear on the Board of Supervisors from several different forces. An active group of preservationists—The Friends of the Blue Ridge Parkway—and an active, organized group of citizens have been pushing for low density zoning and open space requirements on these viewsheds. An equally active group of homebuilders and developers have been pushing for higher density zoning on these properties. Unfortunately, there was not a level playing field. The nonprofit groups and citizen groups were not involved in this process at an early enough stage to really be effective. While the zoning ordinance was being rewritten and the zoning maps revised groups interested in protection of the Parkway were unaware of the process and therefore silent. On the other hand, the homebuilders association and the development community were well informed and actively participated in the early stages of this process. Some of the responsibility for this falls on the shoulders on the County, but some must also be taken by these nonprofit groups. The zoning process did not take place in a vacuum. There were public meetings, public hearings, and public notices. Community groups need to stay on top of what is happening in their neighborhoods. This takes time and energy, but the best time to get involved in the decision-making process is early when you can influence decisions rather than being in the untenable position of trying to get decisions changed.

# Hope Diamond
*Richard Posner*

My first run-in with the LAPD was in the summer of 1948. A motorcycle policeman with siren blaring pulled my parents over for speeding through the intersection of Adams and Normandie. Once the cop caught a glimpse of my mother's huge pregnant stomach, however, he remounted the Harley, turned the siren back on, and motioned us to follow. At 6:22 a.m. the next morning, August 16, at Cedars of Lebanon Hospital, the day Babe Ruth died, I was born.

Who were these reckless drivers? My father was in the newspaper business. He and his father sold papers on a South Chicago street corner until Second World War defense work brought them to South-Central Los Angeles. Once her sons were out of diapers, my mother taught kindergarten in Watts for twenty-two years.

That was then. Now is "verdict season" in the City of Angels, a time of year marked by dread and hope as we brace for the next round in the trials of our two most famous unlucky motor vehicle operators, Rodney G. King and Reginald O. Denny. Heartwarming tales of "Just the facts, ma'am" police work, and family perseverance have long since been eclipsed by the kind of superstition and circumstance associated with the Santa Ana winds and the swallows' return to Capistrano. "Verdict season," which falls between Opening Day and the World Series, goes back to the time of the 1910 bombing of the *L.A. Times*, the 1940s' Black Dahlia and Sleepy Lagoon murder cases, and the 1965 Watts Rebellion. It is a period of random violence and white-knuckle terror followed by paroxysms of civic hand-wringing. Bicycling downtown this morning past clusters of homeless people encamped between Spring and Hope, streets which run parallel but do not meet, was yet another reminder of the helplessness this season has come to characterize.

For ideological reasons which at the time I did not understand, my parents made a practice of always being one of the last Caucasians to live in primarily African American, Asian, and Hispanic neighborhoods. This meant that as soon as I was old enough to walk, I got caught in the crosshairs of other people's race, class, and gender hatreds: first at 61st Street Elementary School, then at Audubon Junior High School, and later at Dorsey High School.

About the time the Dodgers arrived from Brooklyn, family visions for a just society were becoming overshadowed by daily struggles to keep a roof over our heads and food on the table. Although raised in a Jewish household, my childhood religious education became a daily preoccupation with survival. Each morning I would pray to arrive at school without getting knifed by neighborhood punks. Each afternoon I would pray to be allowed to complete my paper route without getting knocked upside the head or robbed by corner dope dealers. Evening prayer asked for a least one-half hour of streetball without being run over by oncoming traffic. That Darwin and Houdini were my patron saints should come as no surprise.

School, paper route, and blacktop stickball were necessary evils. My salvation was weekend softball played on real live grass with people not out to harm me. The Rancho Cienega Playground softball diamond, since renamed Jackie Robinson Field, was a demilitarized zone. It provided our neighborhood with a common ground for the temporary cessation of hostilities.

In *Take Time for Paradise*, the late Commissioner of Baseball, A. Bartlett Giamatti, wrote about the diamond as "a green expanse, complete and coherent, shimmering, carefully tended, and garden." All I knew was that I was in heaven each Saturday, patrolling center field and scanning the horizon for enemy fly balls, while getting intoxicated by the sweet smell of clover and fescue beneath my feet. My only prior big lawn experience was the spongy, manicured carpet of the Hollywood Jewish Cemetery, where on alternate Sundays I would accompany my parents to perform the old Hebrew custom of placing three stones on my grandparents' graves. When they lay me to rest, let the gravestone read: "He was a homeboy who defied many stereotypes. His people were neither absentee landlords nor any relation to the New Jersey Posners who sold hair straightener and skin toner products to African Americans. He came from two generations of mystical German rabbis and Russian socialists whose small hands bore no relation to the size of their genitalia."

At the onset of puberty, while other young art students diligently copied old masters such as Rembrandt and Durer, my work took off in another direction. I regularly bicycled to the L.A. Coliseum several hours before Dodger home games to collect the autographs of Hodges and Snider, masters whose signature I would later replicate on Little League teammates' gloves. While admittedly and activity pursued without the expressed written consent of Major League Baseball, in my defense I can only say that it was a skill briefly practiced for one season in the hope that it would compensate for a baseball prowess that consisted of a weak bat, a rubber arm, and gimpy legs. Hope does spring eternal.

I was across the street from the L.A. Coliseum, at the University of Southern California on April 29, 1992, the day the riots erupted. As a visiting artist in the School of Fine Arts, I had just presented my sculpture class with an environmental design assignment to address the isolation between USC and the surrounding South Central neighborhood. A vacant lot at the intersection of Hoover and 35th Streets was chosen as the location for this exercise in "town/gown" interaction.

When I relocated back to South Central L.A. in 1990, after being away from the area since 1965, I could not believe how wide the social, physical and economic divisions between the neighborhood and campus had grown. Few bridges and even less common ground seemed to exist. The "town/gown" boundary had become an armed Maginot Line with little or no demilitarized space in between.

"If you build it, he will come." The genesis for making a "stained grass" window grew out of a conversation a decade earlier with Japanese artist, Shoji Kurokami, who at the time was my studio assistant. While tossing a softball back and forth during a work break, we discussed baseball and language word play. Shoji commented how Japanese alphabetic structure makes it difficult to discern English sounds such as *v, th, l,* and *r,* which do not appear in Japanese. He had just read W. S. Kinsella's *Shoeless Joe* and suggested we build a "praying field." It took ten years to find the right spot.

The project, originally planned for the first weekend in May, was postponed when violence erupted a few miles away at the intersection of Florence and Normandie. "I stood in Venice on the Bridge of Sighs and saw a palace on one end and a prison on the other," wrote Lord Byron (*Childe Harold's Pilgrimage,* c. IV st.1). I stood on Venice Boulevard and saw the flames of Fedco on one end and a Korean minimart is ashes on the other. Billowing waves of smoke the size of Kansas twisters wafted overhead. The clouds were neither a sign that a new pope had been chosen, nor an indication that I was about to be whisked away to Oz.

By the time the fires subsided, school was over. Finals were canceled. Students were gone and most faculty had fled town. The handful of my class who remained however, felt a strong conviction to follow through with our plan.

In response to the sight of our City as a living hell, a *Hope Diamond* was made at the corner of 35th and Hoover Streets. We wanted to provide television news helicopters something to shoot besides arson and looting. With bold "Trojan color" cardinal red and gold letters forming the palindrome LIVENOTONEVIL inscribed within its ring, *Hope Diamond* was a temporary earthwork and softball diamond where everyone could steal home. Painted as National Guardsmen still patrolled the streets, this 150-foot-by-375-foot landscape painting was visible for forty-eight hours over May 30 and 31, the Memorial Day weekend.

In order to make a permanent record of this ephemeral artwork, a time lapse camera documented three weeks of design, fabrication, and dissolution activity from the rooftop vantage point of a nearby twelve-story building. The movie condensed twenty hours of surveying, striping and painting with biodegradable turf pigment (donated by the Decratrend Corporation), a two-hour softball game (complete with an 18-carat outfield made by neighborhood kids holding carrot silhouettes), and twenty-one days of gradual dissolution from lawn mowing, intermittent rain, and general public use, into a six-minute film. It chronicles the transformation of a vacant lot into a regulation softball diamond, and its subsequent reversion back into a diamond-in-the-rough.

*Hope Diamond* was an oasis. It was a garden for contemplation and a place for athletic activity where being was as important as playing, cooperation took precedence over competition, and neither winning nor losing were as important as just playing. A whistled rendition of the National Anthem preceded the ceremonial throwing out of the first ball by "Dizzy Dean" Matteson, the Dean of the School of Fine Arts. The motley crew of people who showed up chose sides on the basis of odd-year versus even-year birth dates, then took places on what several participants described as "The World's Largest Diamond."

Huge diamonds do not always bode good fortune. According to Guiness, the original Hope Diamond, the famous gem mined in 17th-century India and now in the Smithsonian Institution, known as much for its beauty as for the bad luck associated with its ownership, was rumored to be around the neck of Marie Antoinette when she lost her head. The people's *Hope Diamond*, if nothing more than an exercise in visual alchemy, at least momentarily transformed the infamous jewel's legendary curse into a blessing.

*Hope Diamond* did not lure hundreds of Angelenos out of their armed response homes or air-conditioned vehicles. Neighborhood folks were discouraged from seeing it by overzealous campus parking lot attendants who demanded a $5 entry fee per car, with no exceptions. Even the several helicopters that briefly hovered overhead quickly flew off in search of fast-breaking action news.

*Hope Diamond* did provide a revelation for Jesse Velasquez. The grounds keeper who methodically striped baseball and football lines at USC home games for the past 20 years, Jesse approached the

*Hope Diamond* with some trepidation. Several weeks earlier, he was caught between strong-arm administration demands that staff remain on campus during the riot in order to protect USC property, and family concerns for his own health and safety. His preoccupation with school and family matters disappeared, however, the moment Jesse saw the *Hope Diamond* from the ledge of the adjacent building roof. Slapping both hands over his open jaw, he gasped, "Holy Mother of God." With an ear-to-ear Cheshire cat grin, Jesse looked at my students and beamed, "We did this?"

Signs of hope, always difficult to find, are particularly elusive during "verdict season."

---

Richard Posner was born in South Central Los Angeles, where he attended Dorsey High School. Upon completion of four years of alternative service in Appalachia as a Vietnam War Conscientious Objector, Posner received his MFA from California College of Arts and Crafts in 1976. An NEA Fellow (1977), Fulbright Scholar (1980), McKnight (1989), Jerome (1990), and Pollock-Krasner Foundation Award (1994) recipient, Posner's work is in the permanent collections of the Victoria and Albert Museum, the Metropolitan Museum of Art, the Smithsonian Institution, the Corning Museum, the Exploratorium, and the Craft and Folk Art Museum, as well as in private collections throughout North America, Europe, Scandinavia, and Japan. Posner's numerous percent for art commissions are in state and federal buildings across California, Oregon, and Washington. His *Consumer's Lobby*, the main entry for the U.S. Food and Drug Administration in Bothell, Washington, received the General Services Administration 1992 Design Excellence Award. Posner has been a Fellow at the MacDowell Colony, Yaddo, The Blue Mountain Center, The Ragdale Foundation, and the Virginia Center for Creative Arts. Posner's work has been published in newspapers and magazines including *Art In America, Time, High Performance, New Art Examiner, Landscape Architecture, American Craft, The New York Times, The Washington Post, The Village Voice,* and *The L.A. Weekly*. Posner is the author of *Intervention & Alchemy: A Public Art Primer* and numerous essays about art and culture.

# The Public Spirit of the Recreation Demonstration Area Program

*Bonj Szczygiel*

The Blue Ridge Parkway, host of the 1993 Linear Parks conference, was a project conceived during the 1930s depression. A multifaceted endeavor, the Parkway was meant to help the Appalachian economy while offering an opportunity for touring motorists to experience the mountain scenery and history—pleasantly motoring at safe speeds with preserved viewsheds to be appreciated. Given the intended spirit of the Parkway experience, and of this conference, it would seem appropriate to discuss another multifaceted New Deal program; a recreation area building program that also carried with it the typical New Deal double-edge of economic recovery and social impact, called the Recreation Demonstration Area program.

The Recreation Demonstration Area (RDA) program exemplifies the hands-on, take-charge attitude shared by President Roosevelt and members of his "brain trust." Ironically the program remains today as one of the administration's more obscure efforts. RDAs were federally-developed recreational parks with a strong social and economic mission. Intended as eventual gifts to the states, legal ownership of the parks were transferred soon after completion. As those transfers took place, RDA names were changed to state park designations and the program faded in the nation's memory. Today the number of people who recognize RDA as one of Roosevelt's "alphabet programs" are unquestionably few. Yet Conrad Wirth, organizer of the CCC state park program and director of the National Park Service (NPS) from 1951 to 1964 called the RDA program "one of the really successful New Deal programs . . ." (1980, 176).

The goal of the RDA program was nothing short of remedying the economic, environmental and social malfunctioning of a given community. Even the program's title indicates the strong-arm approach in teaching, or *demonstrating*, how to improve nonproductive land-use practices in this country. To accomplish this, the program acquired submarginal farm land or otherwise nonproductive, overused land. The people living on the barren land were removed—either resettled into one of the administration's subsistence homesteads or simply compensated for the purchase and asked to vacate. The "retired" land was then rehabilitated and developed by CCC or WPA workers into a recreation area targeted for use by local underprivileged urban children and families. Proximity to cities was a key factor in RDA location.[1] The idea was that with proper land-use management, entire regions could be reformed—productivity given back to the people and the land alike. One program official at a regional meeting of state park work in 1935 put it this way, "By emphasizing the proper use of land and natural resources as the basis of a sound agricultural and industrial economy" we can bring about "a new approach to the correction of social and economic maladjustments of many sorts" (NPS 1935, 20). The plan was grand from its very inception, and yet there were only 31 RDAs developed in this country. An approximation is that for every ten state parks developed or improved during the New Deal, there was one RDA (Merrill 1981, 108-195). The purpose of this paper is to describe the RDA program in terms of its goals, management and eventual scope; and to look at RDA built form as it responded to those programmatic standards.

## The RDA Program

The RDA program was conceived one year after Franklin Delano Roosevelt took office. Concerned with land planning issues, especially submarginal farm issues, the government on February 28, 1934, set aside 25 million dollars of its Federal Emergency Relief Administration (FERA) funds for a land utilization program. The "Land Program" was the result. In a 1934 memo that captured the spirit of this broadly optimistic program, the director of the Land Program wrote, "Whenever land is being misused or whenever land may be put to a different and more beneficial use, such land may be acquired under the Land Program of the Federal Emergency Relief Administration" (National Archives, R.G. 79, File 601). After the 1934 dust storm, when skies were solid with Great Plains grit, the Land Program was yet another reassuring symbol of the federal government's new caretaker role. In one broad sweep, the Land Program was designed to purchase abused land, improve the lives of the land owners (by relocating them to more productive land), improve the lives of the nearby urban "industrially stranded" population groups while simultaneously cutting local government costs and teaching the country how to manage land via experimental projects that would serve as "repeatable demonstrations." No small task was before the Land Program as it tried to juggle multiple interests from both the Interior Department and the Department of Agriculture, each agency attempting to get a piece of this land-purchasing action (figure 1).

The NPS was granted Land Program funds for the development of four types of recreation demonstration projects:

Figure 1. The Land Program's Organizational Chart

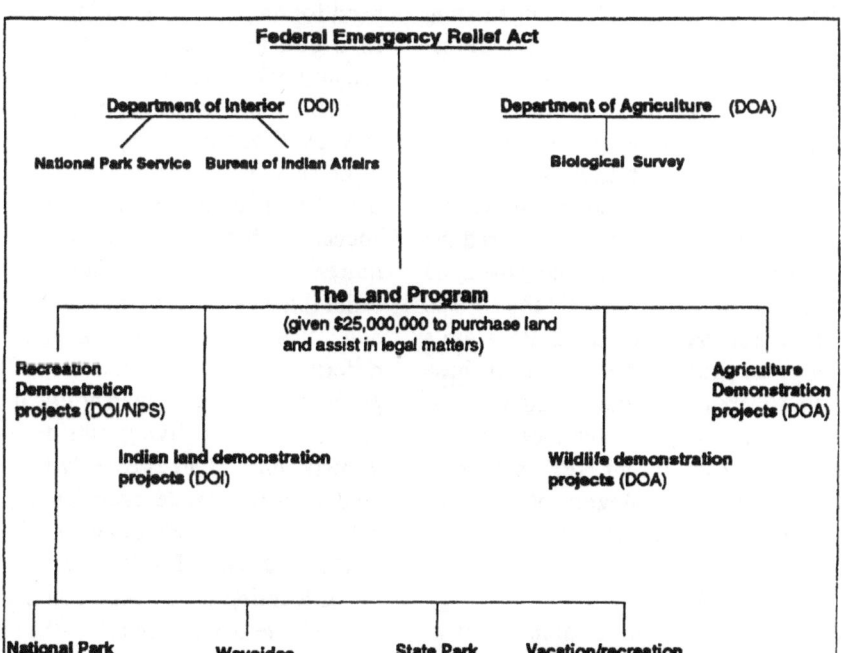

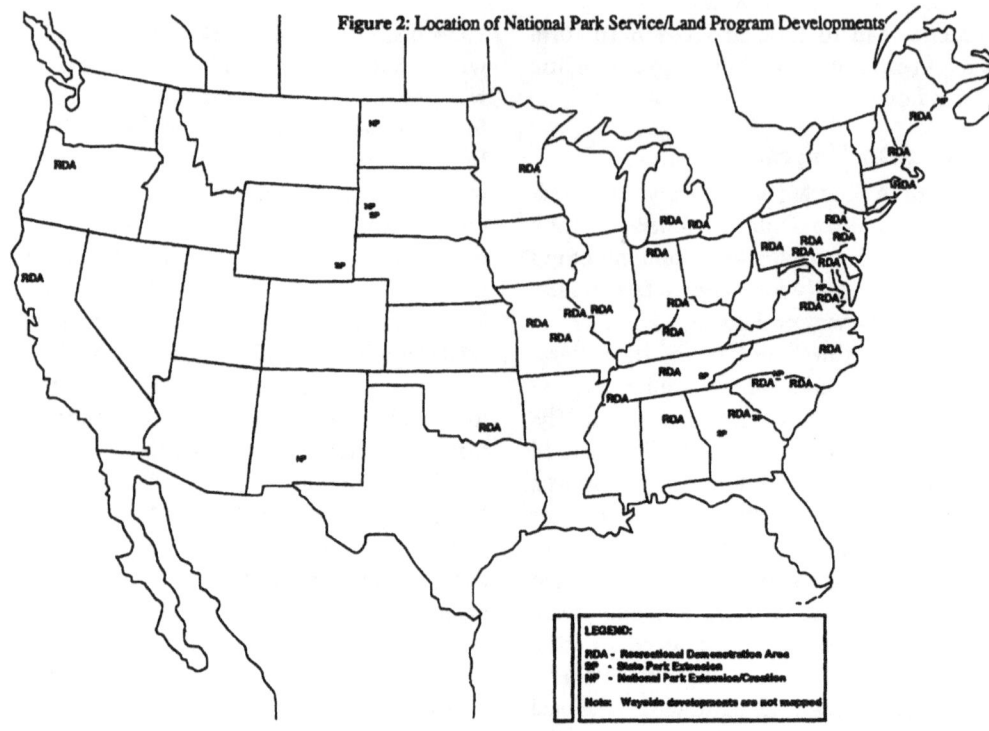

Figure 2: Location of National Park Service/Land Program Developments

1) areas for existing or proposed national parks, monuments and historic areas, 2) development of waysides along existing or proposed highways, 3) state scenic area/park extensions, and 4) the program's main thrust —development of vacation and recreation areas. Although all four types of land use demonstrations were called "recreation demonstration area projects," the last category alone fully answered the multipurpose challenge issued by the Land Program. In no other form did the NPS so ardently embrace the Land Program's ideology as in the development of these vacation/recreation demonstration areas. Accordingly, throughout this paper, "RDA" does not refer to all four NPS categories, but only to the last category of vacation/recreation demonstration developments.

**RDA Locations**

Areas selected for the establishment of Land Program projects, including RDAs, were based on state and federal land classifications which indicated relative need for an *adjustment* of land-use. And, in a confidential statement issued in January 1934, Land Program director John Landsill noted that because of the "demonstrational" aspect of the projects, sites had to be selected in terms of not only need, but also in terms of expected levels of success. Therefore, less-publicized requirements such as standards of living, relief loads, local governmental finances, and other economic and social factors quietly entered into the site selection process. Unaware of such political undercurrents, farmers living outside the previously selected areas eagerly listed their land with real estate agencies hoping to catch the eye of federal agents (National Archives, R.G. 79 File 201). The mechanics of locating the 31 RDAs was to have worked interdepartmentally—the regional directors of the Land Program, established in offices across the nation (to confirm the submarginal quality of land), worked with the district officers of the NPS (who determined the recreational appropriateness of land), and state and local agencies (who agreed to accept eventual ownership of the development) to select potential sites for RDA development. Final land-purchasing decisions were made by the Washington office of FERA. Aside from this democratic approach, those areas of the country beset with the worst ecological conditions received the greatest RDA concentrations.

A glance at a map of RDA locations points to some of the country's environmental tender spots (figure 2). A notable exception to this general rule is the environmentally devastated Dust Bowl region; Texas to North Dakota. This area is barely represented in RDA development because there lacked the population to justify the expenditure (National. Archives, R.G. 79, File 601-12). Of the six NPS/Land Program purchases in this area, only one was for RDA development—Lake Murray, Oklahoma; the other five areas were used to "round-out" existing NPS lands, to fatten-up state park holdings and to create a new national park—Theodore Roosevelt National Park—which included 63,000 acres of Teddy Roosevelt's Elk Horn Ranch (where his 'Rough Riders" were reportedly organized). Purchased at $2.00/acre, this land was far below the average $10—$25.00 per acre cost paid by the Land Program in other sections of the country.

A second area to host NPS/Land Program development was the north central lowlands—the corn belt including Indiana, Illinois and Missouri. Subsistence farmers, trying to make a living on sandy, nutrient-poor soils and other submarginal lands, saw their work spiral further downward in the 1930s pre-depression agricultural crisis. They continued to lose their farms to bankruptcy as the depression hit full stride. Six RDAs are testament to those hard times.

Pennsylvania has a total of five RDAs, a record development for one state. Their presence points to the state's previously strong industrial base subdued by both the 1890s and 1930s depressions (Pennsylvania and Michigan, which hosts two RDAs, registered unemployment figures of 25% and 44% respectively, during the 1890s depression) (Grant 1983, 8). Pennsylvania also had a long history of denuding its woodlands, and amidst the over-timbered hillsides, tucked into the many watergaps and valleys, struggled farmers lived in virtual isolation. Beyond its economic and environmental qualifications, Pennsylvania also had a functioning state park system which may have attracted RDA program attention; "previous organization" presented one less administrative headache for the NPS. [2] It may also be presumed that the two-term Governor, ex-forester Gifford Pinchot, helped to present his state as a ready and willing candidate for federal funds. Pinchot's biographer describes the Governor as being "consumed" by his efforts to obtain federal relief money for his state. "No governor pounded more consistently or vigorously on Washington's door . . ." (McGreary 1960, 372). As a result all major cities in the state, but one, had an associated RDA.

The 1892 boll weevil infestation can be mapped by its trail of destruction in the Cotton Belt, followed by a trail of Land Program activity. This one Mexican invader fairly succeeded in crippling the Piedmont belt from eastern Alabama to North Carolina, though it took the agricultural crisis of the 1920s to finally devastate the farmers. As part of a general survey of potential recreational sites conducted by the Interior Department

Figure 3. Typical NPS camp design.
From *Park & Recreation Structures* by Albert H. Good (1990).

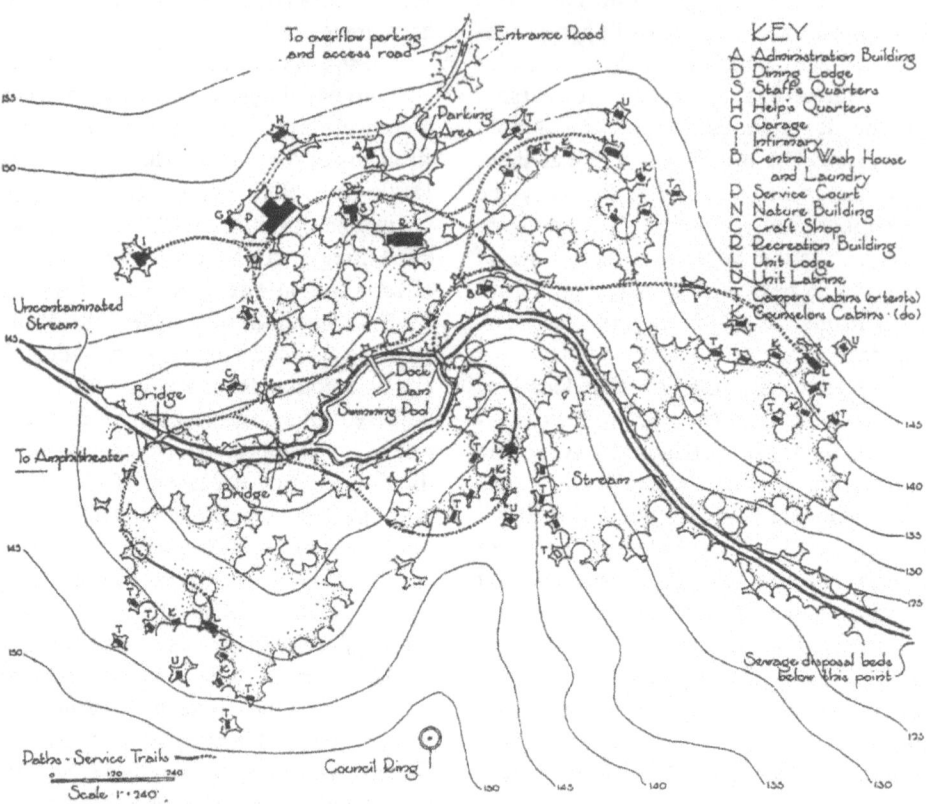

A LARGE ORGANIZED CAMP ALONG A DAMMED STREAM

(circa 1934), the southern Piedmont region was described as possessing one-fifth of the country's entire submarginal farm lands:

> In this region we find a common problem; complete bankruptcy of the former prosperous social and economic systems; impoverished population stranded on poor land trying to grow cotton and corn; impotent local governments helpless to provide adequate health, schooling and other public facilities; loss of soil fertility and gullying of land through uncontrolled erosion. (National Archives, R.G. 79, File 601-12)

In the Cotton Belt are five RDAs, two state park additions and one national park extension.

The rest of the RDAs are less concentrated—aside from the Appalachian projects including work along the Blue Ridge Parkway (Virginia & North Carolina) and in Shenandoah National Park (Virginia)—and represent efforts by individual states to get a federal project, and federal funds, in their midst.

The importance of having previously organized state park systems helps to explain the lack of RDA developments west of the Mississippi. Just as that part of the country had seen little need for Fresh

Air camps 50 years earlier, a movement with many similarities to the RDA program prevalent in eastern and central states (Szczygiel 1992, 29), so it would be years later when western states of limited urban development, vast open space and perhaps a national park in their backyard found little need for organized recreation in the form of RDAs. There are only two west-coast RDAs: Silver Creek, Oregon—now Silver Falls State Park—and Mendocino RDA, California—now Mendocino Woodlands Outdoor Center.

## RDA Built Form

As mentioned earlier, RDAs were meant to lose their federal associations. From their inception they were to be turned over to their respective states for maintenance, possible further development and inclusion in the state park system. For almost all RDAs that transfer occurred between 1943-1945. There is one notable exception: 5,500 acres of Catoctin RDA in Maryland were chosen as a presidential retreat by Roosevelt in 1942, a place he called "Shangri-la." It enabled him to escape from, yet be close to, the capitol during WW II. Later, President Eisenhower changed the name to Camp David. [3] Whatever the degree of envelopment by the National Capitol Park System, or the state park systems, RDAs remained physically distinct through the NPS concept of "organized camps."

Organized camps are the brainchild of the NPS even though group camping had been a fixed element in the world of private recreation since the mid-1800s. Those earlier, privately sponsored camp buildings were mostly of the barracks type, usually lined in an orderly fashion as if to enforce a regimentation of spirit. Critics of this earlier style of camp were quick to note these buildings were often accompanied by an equally strict organization of daily activities for the youngsters. Tongue-in-cheek, NPS director Albert Good described the deficits of that overorganized style, "It will," he wrote, "sometime be recorded that regimentation of camping wrote its own death warrant on a day when a leader of extraordinary genius hit upon the idea of a mass brushing of all the teeth in camp to a kind of dance routine and timing" (1938, Part III, 4). So what was the preferred alternative to camp design? It seemed to be a throw of the dice. "Dice throw" planning is the characterization tagged on NPS organized camp layouts. The effort was by no means as casual as the name implies but rather weighted heavily by consideration of group dynamics; the preservation or re-creation of the wooded character; the desire to reinforce the individuality of the child, and always, an attempt to tread lightly on the land.[4] The seemingly careless layout of the buildings was the result of careful analysis. Dignity of the land and of the human experience are addressed in the gentle clustering of cabins and the unobtrusive location of the camp's more functional buildings, such as dining hall and infirmary, to the sleeping cabins (figure 3).

Typically each RDA was comprised of 2 to 5 separate camps. The camps contained main staff and support buildings, connected by narrow paths to clusters of sleeping cabins, or units. Each unit could accommodate from 18 to 36 campers. Further enhancing the wilderness effect, the sleeping cabins were small (accommodating only two or four persons), had no bathroom facilities, kitchens or closets and remained basically one-room, unheated structures.

The subtle touch of design was also applied to the spatial relationship of each individual sleeping cabin. The cabins were discreetly placed. At no time will you find them too close, or facing one another, or too far away from each other. They will instead be slightly askew, subtly turned away so that when the young campers walk out of their cabin they will see nature, not another building, yet never feel abandoned. Paths connecting the cabins with other units respond to the land, as do the approach roads into the RDA. If the dictum "nature abhors a straight line" is true, it was also true for the NPS. But the designs are obviously more meaningful that; they are an exaltation of nature and a careful cradling of the individual. These clusters of small buildings, with their sensitive, low-impact placement on the land were, I believe, a response by the NPS to create a rewarding, enriching experience for the urban youth. The design of NPS organized camps assumed responsibility for those overwhelmed by a harsh urban society, it would have been foreign for them to do less.

The architecture of the camp buildings was also in keeping with the larger goals of the organized camp experience—where the uniqueness of place (and therefore design) was taken seriously and where local materials were used to minimize intrusion on the land. "NPS rustic" architecture, that which blends and harmonizes with nature, was meant to reflect the uniqueness of the land and of the individual. Each RDA development was treated with architectural integrity; to date I have not witnessed a duplication of architectural detail in any of the camps visited. While specific regional identities are less pronounced, variety in detail within each individual RDA was the norm. Within an organized camp, architectural variation from unit to unit was usually subtle— whether in treatment, placement or number of windows, porches, doorways etc.— variation upon a theme seems to have been the guiding force. Yet each individual cabin, no matter how small, was conferred dignity. NPS designers were not cookie-cutters; for all the dogma encircling the rustic style, [5] there existed a refreshing latitude of nonconformity.

That which gives RDAs character— the organized camps—is also the bane of their continued existence. Each camp, usually located in the park's most primitive area, may have over 50 small, separate buildings. Each building, if previously unrepaired, has fifty years of wear and weather on them. If unused, the remote location of the cabins allows vandals to go undetected. A building's derelict condition may cause alarm for park superintendents concerned for the general public's welfare. Some parks have closed public access to their cabins, others closely monitor any activity in the vicinity. In times of slashed budgets, when state parks are barely able to keep the heavily used areas clean and in repair, the loose collection of many little buildings tucked into the far reaches of park wilderness does not offer solace. Some RDA cabins have been razed, others will soon follow. On a more positive note, a recent survey of RDA/park superintendents revealed that the majority of RDA camps (16 out of the 28 responses) have units in good shape and in good use. Campers remark about the unique architecture, the quiet and privacy afforded them and the beautiful locations. People who enjoy and anticipate the primitive conditions are pleasantly surprised by the graciousness of the accommodations and surroundings. Three state parks have turned operation of individual camps over to private agencies for lease and maintenance. That situation seems to work well as a way of diverting the costs from already strapped state park agencies. Given that park superintendents are saddled daily with the responsibility of building maintenance, their overall reaction to the hundreds of RDA structures was quite positive. More

## End Note

On a visit to Raccoon Creek State Park, outside of Pittsburgh, a few years ago I wandered into the remnants of an abandoned RDA organized camp. There, in the calm of an overgrown meadow, sat about 20 small cabins. Each was turned slightly from the other, some faced a deep, tree-clad ravine, others addressed the bright expanse of meadow. At first glance the small buildings seemed in good architectural health—a few crooked shutters, an occasional boarded window—but essentially looked as they had almost sixty years ago. But with closer scrutiny, their casual appearance was a shell. The buildings no longer served any function. Their repair had fallen behind, the unusual chestnut log foundations held firm but moisture had rotted interior floor boards. Roofs needed to be replaced. What should be done with these gems in the forest? Should the symbols of a nation at its peak of creativity and desperation continue to be ignored, or worse destroyed? Raccoon Creek recently decided to begin restoring their antique structures and promote their active use. Reactions are mixed at other state parks. Yet whatever the fate of these buildings, their structural fortitude over the years speaks well of their builders. The legacy of the Recreation Demonstration Area program lives, though quite anonymously, within their walls.

## NOTES

1. The determination of national parks was stated in a 1934 NPS press release to be "primarily set aside because of superlative scenic beauty, natural phenomena, or to preserve archeological treasures and rare wilderness features." Prior to the '30s depression, state parks also tended to follow this pattern. Their locations traditionally were determined by the unique and attractive quality of the landscape regardless of their remoteness to population centers. RDA site selection was in direct contrast to those policies. Instead, it was mandated that sites be within 50 miles from an urban core and that the land be nonproductive, non-sustainable or otherwise overused and therefore considered valueless.

2. When asked for the criteria in selection of RDA sites, one NPS representative remarked, off-the-cuff, that the most important consideration for RDA site selection was a state agency "willing to accept the responsibility for maintenance and operation . . ." (NPS 1935, 22).

3. Camp David is the most famous of the former RDAs—a place so mysterious and important that even Andy Rooney, of *60 Minutes* fame, attempted a break-in of the compound (October 10, 1993 airing). He was firmly ousted by the Marines.

4. In a chart illustrating factors involved in organized camp location and development, the NPS stated their objectives regarding site selection, development, personnel, and types of activities. According to the chart, all these consideration were to act in concert to produce "A healthy, happy productive member of society" (Good 1938, 120).

5. As recently as the March 1991 edition of Landscape Architecture magazine, James Krohe, Jr. found opportunity to take a swipe at NPS "parkitecture," further referred to as a "sticks and stones" style that was nothing more than a variant of the log cabin (70).

## REFERENCES

Cutler, Phoebe. 1985. *The Public Landscape of the New Deal*. New Haven: Yale University Press.

Eells, Eleanor. 1986. *History of Organized Camping: The First 100 Years*. Martinsville, IN: American Camping Association.

Good, Albert H. 1938. *Park and Recreation Structures*. 1990 reprint with introduction by Laura Soulliere Harrison. Boulder: Graybooks.

Grant, H. Roger. 1983. *Self-Help in the 1890s Depression*. Ames, IA: The Iowa State University Press.

McGeary, Martin Nelson. 1960. *Gifford Pinchot, Forester-Politician*. Princeton, NJ: Princeton University Press.

Merrill, Perry H. 1981. *Roosevelt's Forest Army: A History of the Civilian Conservation Corps 1933-1942*. Montpelier, VT: Perry H. Merrill.

National Park Service. 1935. "Meeting of Fifth Regional Staff: State Park Conservation Work." Unpublished manuscript. St. Louis, MO.

Schuyler, David. 1986. *The New Urban Landscape*. Baltimore: The Johns Hopkins University Press.

Szczygiel, Bonj. 1992. "The Recreation Demonstration Area Project of the New Deal." Unpublished master's paper. University Park, PA: The Pennsylvania State University, Department of Landscape Architecture.

Tilden, Freeman. 1962. *The State Parks: Their Meaning in American Life*. New York: Alfred A. Knopf.

Tweed, William C., Laura E. Soulliere, Henry G. Law. 1977. "National Park Service Rustic Architecture: 1916-1942." Unpublished report. National Park Service Western Regional Office, Division of Cultural Resource Management.

Wirth, Conrad L. 1980. *Parks, Politics, and the People*. Norman: University of Oklahoma Press.

## GOVERNMENT DOCUMENTS

Information regarding the RDA program was obtained through records held at the National Archives, Washington, D.C. in the Preliminary Inventory of the Record of the National Park Service (Record Group 79), RDA Program Files: General, Administrative, and Personnel and Reports. The information gathered at those sources supplied most of the RDA and Land Program data at the national level.

# Case Study: Devil's Courthouse Trail
*Harry L. Baker*

## LOCATION
The trail head begins at Devil's Courthouse parking overlook at parkway milepost 422.4.

## ELEVATION
The trail ascends from an elevation of 5462 feet at the overlook to a summit elevation of 5740 feet. Trail length is over 2300 feet. The climb is about 278 feet.

## GEOLOGY
Land forms that make up this site within the Great Pisgah Range were moved westward over 180 miles in geosynclinic folds by upthrusts and overthrusts of the metamorphosed beds of sea sediments by forces of the African Plate grinding against the North American Plate. This took place over a period of 240 million years. At the present time of the geologic clock this formation called Devil's Courthouse exposes a rock face of granitic gneiss.

## PHYSIOGRAPHY
Our site sits on the south slope of the Great Pisgah Range within a massive triangular plateau averaging 5400 feet elevation. This plateau also includes the Tennessee Ridge.

## FLORA
What is left of a Dominant Spruce-Fir Climax Community stands derelict either side of the trail as it climbs the north slope and ridge line to the summit. Acid deposition and the Balsam Wooly Aphid of the 1980s, in conjunction with extreme periods of drought have left their mark. Associated communities of this area include but are not limited to the following:

| | |
|---|---|
| Yellow Rirch | *Betula Allegheniensis* |
| Mountain Ash | |
| Catawba Rhododendron | *Catawbeiense Rhododendron* |
| Fetter Bush | *Pieris Floribunda* |
| Mountain Laurel | *Kalmia Latifolia* |
| Service Berry | *Amelanchier Arborea* |

Despite the impact of the Aphids these Balsams are popping up from seed by natural regeneration and someday will regain a niche in these mountains.

## PARKWAY TRAILS
A parkway trail should be a vehicle of access to sequential points of visual and interpretive resources experiences. A trail is planned on the one hand and is a spontaneous experience on the other—but is always supported by parking. Trails add to our resources access despite the misuse and overuse impacts of increasing numbers of visitors. And they must always be properly signed. We offer these trails for your personal experience but we also expect your experience to be as a visitor we invite.

## A CULTURAL RESOURCE
Resources access also includes myth and its interpretive potential. In a time before the white man had strewn his place names over every hill and hollow of the Great Pisgah Range only Cherokee legend and a natural harmony cloaked these lofty highlands.

As a cultural resource Cherokee Myth adds a sensory experience to the awareness of Devil's Courthouse:

> The mythical giant Tsul-Ka-Lu (called JUDACULLA by the whites) has ethnological associations with the area. The myth goes that when Tsul-Ka-Lu was

first seen by this mother-in-law she reacted in repulsion. Infuriated he sought refuge in the high craggies of Devil's Courthouse where he spent his time within his council house and dancing grounds deep within the rocks of the cliff.

Today no cave of any particular order exists to our knowledge within this formation. But who is to say that such a myth had no foundation at some time in antiquity and now has left no evidence but in myth.

What we know is what remains and that the Cherokee had climbed these heights well before the white man.

## PLANNING

Early in the century, if not before, loggers had already reached these noble heights. A logging trail was found in the 1930s climbing the north slope of the Courthouse by the first planners of the Blue Ridge Parkway. In the late 1930s parkway development plans had been started on section 2V. This included the Devil's Courthouse area. In 1933 Stanley Abbott had been assigned to head the Parkway project. Abbott assigned Henrick Van Gelder to Virginia and for North Carolina he assigned Edward Abbuehl, Associate Landscape Architect to work with the Bureau of Public Roads.

Parkway development plans dated 1939 by Ed Abbuehl show preliminary designs for a 14-car parking overlook and pedestrian trail head. A 10-foot shoulder was proposed for a trailway to carry visitors to the top of Devil's Courthouse.

Abbuehl worked closely with the Bureau of Public Roads on Graphics and construction of section 2V1 (begun in 1939-completed in 1941). Like the road project Devil's Courthouse overlook was finished with a compacted stone surface.

In December 1941, the war emergency stopped most parkway construction till March of 1955 when Troitino and Brown finished Devil's Courthouse tunnel lining that September. Final paving of our area and overlook was accomplished by October of 1958.

Looking at a development plan dated 1942 we see the constructed parkway and parking overlook. The proposal for Devil's Courthouse trail is seen here.

## THE TRAIL

In the early 1960s a nature trail prospectus and a plan for a pedestrian overlook with sighting devices at the summit was drawn up. Stone masonry for the wall was hauled up the pedestrian trail to the ridge and dumped. A parkway jeep was used to haul these materials to the top. Soon the Masonry wall was in place with viewing devices in the state-of the-art of the 1930s. A good idea—but not one single device was left within the year. Vandals can not be apprehended when regular patrol by rangers is impossible. Yet the wall remained to protect the visitor from hazards of the precipice beyond.

A nature trail marker system was installed on both Devil's Courthouse and Richland-Balsam trails. This marker consisted of a metal information card holder on a pipe anchored in a shallow concrete footing. These disappeared rapidly due to frost action at this elevation on a shallow and loose soil.

## THE WOOLY APHID

While all these small things were taking place at the hands of planners the constant dynamics of natural forces beat about these highlands. The Balsam Wooly Aphid had appeared in the 1950s at Mount Mitchell. At that time the Frazier Fir at the courthouse had not shown infection. But in the late 1970s something eerie was settling over the mountains. An acid deposition from constant fog and rains seemed to cause a critical change in the Balsam immune system. One can still see thousands of Frazier Fir snags sweeping across the highest mountain ridges south of Wagon Road Gap to the Great Smoky Mountains.

This 1980 shot on the Richland-Balsam Trail during the high point of wooly aphid damage shows a typical forest floor of wood shamrock, bracken fern, galax, and associated herbal families. But as the canopy dies as seen on this Devil's Courthouse slide, the excess sunlight begins to foster sun loving plants as briers that proliferate newer plant associations.

## TRAIL SURVEYS ARE MADE

The early 1980s also brought deterioration of the trail itself—a threat to visitor safety. By 1983 things were bad. A large section of the pedestrian overlook wall was gone—lost to winter weathering and vandalism—a potential hazard to visitors on top and to climbers below.

Treadways between stations 8+00 and 12+00 were hazardous. Now the parkway was looking at a major reconstruction of the trail.

Plans to replace the traditional viewing devices on the wall were investigated. By February 1984 regional money was available. The question, however, was whether to rehab the existing trail or relocate because of the excessive grades of 15% - 18%. Robert Steinholtz, Denver Service Center trail expert, who had planned our Tanawha trail at Grandfather Mountain, was called in to look at alternatives of action. Steinholtz made a trip with me to Devil's Courthouse. Using the current standard trail grade maximum of 10% we flagged out alternatives 2 and 3. An alternative 1 would be a rehab of the existing trail. Alternatives 2 and 3 would cross fragile and wet drainage areas and would require elevated board walk construction. Environmental impacts to the hydrological resources and the high costs for boardwalks did not favor these two alternatives.

The final decision pointed to rehab of the existing route as it would also be costly to properly obliterate and replant all abandoned trail segments to prevent continued use.

## THE TRAIL CONTRACT

A complete data calculation of all needed quantities for this rehabilitation was formatted into a proposed contract. The finalized contract was put out for bids by Fall of 1984. Everything beyond station 6+64 up to and including the pedestrian overlook was on contract for rehab.

The parkway accepted a bid of $22,779 for the rehab project. Work was projected to begin October 1, 1984 and to finish by January 28, 1985. The contractor's first objective was to "improve" the trailway beyond station 15+59. He was given permission to take a bobcat loader over halfway up the main ridge widening the existing 2' - 3' trail to a 4' - 6' treadway. A front end loader hauled masonry stone for the wall to station 15+59. The bobcat would take it up trail as far as it could go then the narrow Georgia Buggy took it to the top.

By the end of October, Al Altice, the project engineer came out to the job site to reevaluate project quantities. This resulted in change order No. 1 adding work quantities, and additional time:

1. Additional stone for the wall and a complete repointing of the total wall was approved

2. Additional stone masonry steps were designed and

3. A new item for steel anchor pins was added

The project engineer judged that additional material was necessary and that a thorough reconditioning of the wall pointing was essential. The additional cost was $9,908. The contractor's mason was skilled at matching the existing stone. Once a section was finished a stone capping was placed and evenly bonded into air-entrained mortar. This specification would withstand the hard freeze/thaw cycles at this elevation.

The item for replacement of the viewing plates was put in the contract. Earlier we had found a set of viewing plate blanks in parkway storage. We would supply the finished plates to the contractor. Maybe this time with a little design ingenuity we could help prolong their stay on the wall. We installed the new plates with special bolts anchored through a granite block and countersank in the block. In turn, this block was anchored into the wall, as was the block on the pedestal, with two 5/8" anchor bars.

The wall replacement was installed with No. 6 rebars at 4 foot centers. These rebars were tied with galvanized eight gauge steel wire as shown in the drawings. This new section of wall is still holding. The bronze plates still offer the visitor a trail overlook viewing experience as of the 1930s. The workmanship on the interior steps was acceptable. As we can see the original condition prior to contract repair was not.

The cap stones were a protection that the original wall never had. Mortar between the cap stones was fashioned to drain all run off. The new cap stone would protect the wall against the weather—but as you will later see—this is no protection against vandals. Here is the spur use trail with wash out as seen in 1980. Here is the same problem area as stabilized by this contract in 1984.

Toward the end of November the weather turned bad. Rain and cold weather hampered the contractor's men and equipment and increased harmful impact to the parkway's resources. November the 20th a stop order was signed. A project resume work order was set for April 1, 1985. The winter of 84/85 had been especially rough on the trail. Spring rains came pounding as usual but we were there to witness. By May 1 another time extension was set up to July 1, 1985. A timely meeting of the parkway engineer with the contractor ended with a decision to pave the steep section of the trail with a 2" by 6' topping of asphalt. This would extend the existing asphalt surface, which stopped at station 6+64, up slope to end at station 15+59.

The resulting change order No. 2 added $6,705 to the contract: This amount was to cover the proposed paving. This decision to pave helped solve two longtime problems:

1. The six-foot treadway of asphalt would help protect the most erosive prone section of trail (6+64 -15+59).
2. Paving the steep grade would give better traction and safety for all hikers.

## AFTER THE CONTRACT

At the contract's completion all masonry was in place and the viewing plates were back in place for the first time in over 20 years. The paving had replaced the log water bars as specified in the original contract. A set of short diverter bars were set at intervals along the lower edge of the trail pavement. At a later time maintenance put in asphalt water bars that divert smaller increments of water which rush down the trail during runoff. These also require periodic maintenance. The asphalt water bars in combination with the diverter bars do work much better. Today most of the trail is in good shape. The contract steps near the pedestrian overlook are OK.

A set of random boulder steps are holding up. Log water bars are still in place on the upper segment of trail. The asphalt trail is enduring some edge damage; but for the location—it serves the visitor well. In fact, the visitor tolerates the trails steepness by striking out for the grand destination which is seen from the parking area.

HUMAN IMPACTS

As use increases we know that resources increase in wear, but some frequent users of this area don't seem to exhibit environmental sensitivity. Active recreational use of the area seems to indicate careless disregard for the contracted retaining wall near the top. This wall was installed to maintain a safe treadway for older and handicapped visitors. All cap stones are gone as well as 12 inches of tread surface.

More obvious to view is the vandalism on the main pedestrian wall. In May of this year, a single cap stone was missing from the wall. Just two weeks ago (8/22/93) a total of 13 cap stones were gone. If we ignore this vandalism there is a chance of resource deterioration as we had in the 1980s.

Is this degradation of our resources a problem which might be handled by prescribed use? If not, what must we do? Is it overuse? I strongly encourage a continuing initiative for environmental analyses to determine carrying capacities which these extremely valuable resources of the parkway are able to tolerate.

We should study the social dynamics and behavioral patterns which affect this trail and area, we should investigate recreational trends and logistics that target this area and see what they mean.

Although we ourselves have been less than perfect in protecting this area, we must restate that this is a very special resource, supporting some species that the Park Service remains mandated to protect under legislation.

Use of this area is being impacted with:

1. Off-trail Traffic
2. Illegal Camping
3. Human Waste
4. Litter—caption: "What are you doing here in God's country?"
5. Vandalism
6. Trampling of Plants
7. Pedestrian Traffic Beyond the Wall

What Alternatives short of temporary closure of the area will it take to determine what must be done to sustain the quality of this parkway experience?

The immediate threat from vandalism might be thwarted by the assignment of volunteer monitoring groups to survey the area.

We can rebuild the walls and rehab the trail, but we should and must maintain a sustained recreational area worthy of the society that first put together these words: "to conserve the scenery and the natural and historic objects and the wildlife therein and to provide for the enjoyment of the same in such a manner and by such means as will leave them unimpaired for the enjoyment of future generations." National Park Service Act of 1916

REFERENCES

1. Adkins, Leonard M., 1991, Walking the Blue Ridge.
2. Ara History: Notes in Blue Ridge Parkway library files, 1954, refer to H. C. Wilburn.
3. Lord, William G., 1981, Blue Ridge Parkway Guide, Grandfather Mountain to Great Smokey Mountains National Park (291.9-469 miles).
4. Mooney, James, 1982, Myths of the Cherokee—from 19th and 7th annual reports, B.A.E., Nashville, Tennessee.
5. Parkway's card file (Interpretive Office Library) a. Place names (MP 422.2) b. Parking overlooks, Devil's Courthouse (MP 422.4)
6. Trail Contract Number CX5140-4-2833: (1984-1985) Devil's Courthouse/Richlawn Balsam (Harry Baker—project designer and project supervisor).

# Evolution of Environmental Consciousness and Emergence of an Environmentally Based Linear Parks Movement
*William L. Flournoy, Jr.*

## Brief History of Linear Parks

Since the European colonization of North America, community parks have drawn the public's attention. Environmental consciousness, however, has been an influence and a growing motivation for the development of linear parks for only the last century and a half.

Prior to the mid-1800s, the typical park in North America was the town commons or square. These areas served as a civic focus for their communities, as the centers for government and public gatherings.

By 1858 the basic concepts for park development were being rewritten. In that year, Frederick Law Olmsted, the father of Landscape Architecture as an American profession, and Calvert Vaux submitted a plan for New York's Central Park. The design was founded on the theory that pastoral park scenery, with a gracefully undulating topography and scattered groves of trees, was a powerful antidote to the stress and artificiality of urban life. The plan also advanced the purpose of public health by converting swampy areas into rural landscapes and reducing mosquito breeding potential. Olmsted heightened the sense of calmness in Central Park by carefully separating different landscape types and conflicting uses. For example, he made extensive use of the physical separation of different modes of transportation within the 1,000-acre park.

Over the next 30 years, Olmsted in conjunction with Vaux, landscape architect Charles Eliot, and others, refined the principles of park development and advanced the concepts of linear parks. In 1865 his plan for Cherry Creek Park and Piedmont Way above the College of California in Berkeley included linear characteristics. The plan visualized a pleasure drive and walks along a creek to an overlook at the top of a canyon and would have produced a pleasure drive through the hills between Oakland and the campus.

In 1866, a plan was presented to Brooklyn for Prospect Park. It sought to expand the influences of pastoral parks through an Ocean Parkway connecting Prospect Park to the Coney Island oceanfront, and an Eastern Parkway from the park to the East River.

In 1868, two plans were presented. First, Buffalo's northside park system included a parkway linking the several pastoral parks. Then, a parkway was also proposed to link Riverside, Illinois with Chicago. Riverside was a residential community of Olmsted's design, which incorporated linear open space along the stream system and among neighborhoods.

In 1887 the "Emerald Necklace" was proposed for Boston. It created a 4.5-mile strip park arching around the inner city and linked the Boston Commons with Franklin Park by way of the Back Bay Fens and the Muddy River. By this time, the concept of linear parks had matured to reach beyond that of pastoral parks as a visual and psychological counterpoint to urban development and beyond parkways as a landscaped travel way between parks. Linear parks were at the point of being physically and functionally recognizable as a distinct park type.

The next 80 years saw extensive broadening and deepening in the concepts of linear park development. In 1909, Daniel Burnham presented his Chicago Plan that focused extensively on restoration and reclamation of the Lake Michigan waterfront as linear park and public open space. Burnham's lakefront plans were inspired by Olmsted's work around the city and on the Columbia Exposition. They included lagoons and harbors, a string of offshore islands, and a scenic curving arterial roadway, much of which were created over the following decades.

In 1920 Jens Jensen published a plan for Chicago's Greater West Park system that called for a linear network of parks and open spaces. It was a complement to the earlier Chicago Plan, focusing more on the city west of the lakefront and advocating the concepts of greater use of the natural landscape and native plants.

In 1928, a forester and regional planner named Benton MacKaye wrote *The New Exploration,* which included a prescription to stem urban sprawl at the regional scale. His proposal was for a common public ground forming a linear corridor, around and through localities, well adapted for camping and primitive travel. The 2,147-mile Appalachian Trail, existing from Maine to Georgia, is the manifestation of MacKaye's idea and it exemplifies much of his concept.

In 1909, the Blue Ridge Parkway was conceived as an idea, although it was not born through construction until it could be a Depression Era child. Landscape Architect Stanley Abbott integrated the concepts of curvilinear alignment, limited access, grade-separated crossings, exclusion of commercial traffic, satellite parks, scenic easements, and a consummate blending of natural and cultural features to convert the entire corridor into a single linear park.

A monograph entitled *Securing Open Space for Urban America* was written in 1959 by William H. Whyte for the Urban Land Institute. It describes how a basic open space pattern known as "greenways" could be established before development occurs, thus producing cohesive neighborhoods with open space in between. Whyte continued to write about the concepts of greenways as linear parks in more of his books, including *Cluster Development* (1964) and *The Last Landscape* (1968).

In 1969, the City of Raleigh, NC published, The Park With A City In It, a parks and recreation plan that proposed greenways, and in 1972, Raleigh's City Council accepted a feasibility report and plan for a greenway system. Charles E. Little, in his book *Greenways for America* concluded, "The plan for the Capital Area Greenway... is thought to be the earliest comprehensive local greenway system in the country."

The latter Raleigh plan:

- updated the traditional concepts of linear parks,
- added the emerging knowledge of and interest in ecological system conservation,
- proposed an approach for the continuous perpetuation of the greenway system as the city grew, and
- integrated these with the traditional concepts of linear park development.

## Evolution of Environmental Consciousness

There has been an environmental element to the parks movement for the last 150 years. It was first displayed as health issues, (such as swamp drainage and mosquito eradication), as well as psychological relief from urban development. The movement began to reflect other environmental issues as knowledge of them grew. The common denominators of these evolving environmental issues were their distinctly linear characteristics, and the likelihood that their solution would be pursued through public funding and regulation.

The federal Water Pollution Control Act of 1948 provided technical assistance and funds to strengthen state and local water pollution control programs. The Act focussed only on the construction of sewage systems, without regard for other community needs. Nevertheless, linear sewer for rights-of-way near streams established an important public interest in these corridors.

The National Flood Insurance Program was enacted in 1968 to limit continued development of flood-prone lands, establish construction standards for flood-proofing structures, and authorize subsidized insurance coverage. As communities participated in this program, traditional attitudes about land were changed. No longer could all land be considered to be "created equal"; alternative uses or values had to be found for flood-prone areas. Thus, a public interest was established in keeping flood-prone lands undeveloped.

The Clean Water Act of 1972 strengthened efforts to improve water quality to acceptable minimum standards. One part of the Act, Section 404, established controls over the filling of wetland areas associated with water courses. The Clean Water Act was amended in 1977 to strengthen its standards in pursuit of a "fishable and swimmable" goal for all waters. The Act was further amended in 1988 to include regulation of non-point sources of surface water runoff. As each of these amendments occurred, the relationship between water quality and adjoining land uses was recognized and the public interest in these linear systems was given greater significance.

Over the past 45 years, the development of environmental law has paralleled the continuing development of linear park concepts. This is a natural marriage because both focus on the same geographical area of the landscape, streams and their adjoining lands. In addition to national environmental laws, individual states have also enacted complimentary legislation affecting riparian systems. As layer has been placed upon layer of regulation, the development potential of stream corridors has been reduced and the potential for alternative public uses has increased.

While environmental regulations may keep corridors along streams natural or undeveloped, additional action is required to secure legal public access to those privately owned lands. It has only been within the last decade that increasing numbers of local governments and states have begun the active search for a cost effective way to gain the greatest public benefit from these linear corridors.

## Environmentally Based Linear Parks Movement

Earth Day 1970 is a benchmark for the awakening of the nation to the importance of the environment and the interrelations of ecological systems. Nevertheless, it was not until the *President's Commission On Americans Outdoors Report* in 1986 that nationwide recognition was given to greenways and their environmental, social and cultural importance.

In spite of the growing interest in and knowledge of the environment, the conservation of ecological systems has not evolved as a universal basis for a linear parks movement, which is still driven by the desire for recreational opportunities. The following are a number of structural and institutional weaknesses which need attention before an environmentally based linear parks movement is possible.

1. Environmental program fragmentation is a major stumbling block. Most laws are passed as narrowly focussed, single purpose solutions that do not reflect the interrelations of ecological systems. As a result, programs do not lend themselves to integrated problem solving in conjunction with other types of public programs. Since the strength of linear parks is their ability to accommodate multiple objectives into a public corridor, the environment cannot become a universal basis for such systems until a way is found to integrate environmental programs.

   Short of amending the enabling statutes for all of these programs, there may be no comprehensive solution. A longer term approach would be to identify model programs of multiple objective environmental management in support of linear parks development for aggressive educational and promotional purposes.

2. The mission of linear park system managers can also be a significant deterrent. More often than not, the responsibility for management of linear parks falls to a parks and recreation department. The mission of those departments seldom includes planning for or conducting a conservation program for community-wide ecological systems. This discrepancy limits the potential for an environmentally-based linear parks movement. Two options for eliminating this deterrent are either expanding the missions of parks and recreation departments responsible for linear parks, or dividing the responsibility for linear parks among cooperating departments.

3. Public expectation can advance or restrict development of environmentally-based linear park systems. The first national survey of public perception of park and recreation benefits was reported in *Parks & Recreation* magazine in January 1993. In reporting the 14 most frequently mentioned "community benefits" provided by parks, environmental protection was not present. Neither were any reasonable surrogates, such as open space or nature. They were only mentioned as "individual benefits" of parks, although not highly ranked. This shows that, even though there is broad-based public support for environmental protection, there is no public expectation that linear parks may have a role in conserving ecological systems or the related quality of urban life. If public support is necessary to advance a program through a democratic governmental process, then there is an obvious need and opportunity for public education on the environmental benefits of linear parks before this can be the basis of any movement.

4. Money is required to undertake any major public program, and for better or worse, it can also indicate when a movement is perceived as successful. Considerable amounts of money are being invested in linear parks from numerous local, state and national sources. Yet, the amount of money expended from all sources on linear parks or environmentally-based linear parks has not been identified.

   This is not to suggest that linear parks must have their own dedicated funding source, but there must at least be sufficient bookkeeping and reporting to identify and track the investment in linear parks. This information will indicate the magnitude of the linear parks movement, indicate trends over time, and accommodate the evaluation and planning necessary to continue a more unified movement.

5. Education is key to establishing and maintaining a movement of any type. It is imperative that knowledge be continuously developed and that this knowledge be released from academia in a timely manner. The professionals responsible for the creation of linear parks must receive initial or in-service training to appreciate the full range of characteristics of such systems. Managers must understand the dynamic consequences (ecologic, economic, social and cultural) of their decisions if the complex interrelations of linear parks benefits are to be retained over time. The public must grow to understand in more detail the importance of linear parks to the quality of the environment and urban life. Education at all levels is important to the continuation of the linear parks movement.

## Conclusion

A linear parks movement has been evolving for the last century and a half. Its first third was founded in the rural parks movement and responded with design innovations that linked pastoral parks together and brought linear parks to the community scale. In its second third the movement continued to generate incremental projects based upon existing concepts, but there also was expansion of the theory to the regional and multi-state scale. Its last third has been characterized by renewed interest in the concept of linear parks, and the integration of environmental protection and ecological system conservation into its conceptual basis.

The importance of individual linear parks projects notwithstanding, there is still some question as to the viability of the linear parks movement. There are many examples of linear parks around the world that deserve to be celebrated in all their various forms. There are also many communities and regions that could benefit from linear parks, but may not because of the weaknesses in the movement.

The fundamental theories and concepts of linear parks development are well established. The evolution of environmental consciousness has added essentially linear and interrelated ecological systems as the most current improvement to linear park concepts. Perhaps environmental protection can be the motivation for carrying the linear parks movement forward into the next century; but this can only be accomplished if the entire movement progresses.

The five previously cited weaknesses of an environmentally based linear parks movement can be addresses as a single issue: structural leadership. It is not being provided by the government or private sectors in a manner that encourages the development of environmentally sound linear parks. No entity is planning for or guiding resources to broadscale linear park system development. The educational programs necessary to support the movement are not universally available. Co-ordination among the numerous participants in the linear parks movement is not occurring; and in fact, some participants may not even know they are part of the movement. Clearly the linear parks movement has not been institutionalized, but it must become so if it is to reach its potential for environmental, social and cultural benefit. There is so much to be gained in terms of environmental protection and quality of life, the effort to institutionalize the linear parks movement must be made.

# BIBLIOGRAPHY

"A Focus on Greenway." *National Wetlands Newsletter*, Vol. 10 No. 5, September 1988.

Adams, Lowell W., and Louise E. Dove. *Wildlife Reserves and Corridors in the Urban Environment.* National Institute for Urban Wildlife, 1989.

Adams, Lowell W., and Daniel L. Leedy. *Integrating Man and Nature in the Metropolitan Environment.* National Institute for Urban Wildlife, 1987.

Godbey, Geoffrey, Alan Graefe, and Stephen James. "Reality and Perception." *Parks & Recreation Magazine*, January 1993.

Labaree, Jonathan M. *How Greenways Work, A Handbook on Ecology.* NPS Rivers, Trails and Conservation Assistance Program and the Quebec Labrador Foundation's Atlantic Center for the Environment, 1992.

Little, Charles E. *Greenways for America.* John Hopkins University Press, 1990.

*Report and Recommendations to the President of the United States,* President's Commission on American Outdoors, December 1986.

Whyte, William H. *Securing Open Space for Urban American.* The Urban Land Institute, 1959.

# The Historic Cultural Landscape and an Expanded Vision of Park

*Thomas Yahner and Daniel Joseph Nadenicek*

## Introduction

The everyday landscape in all parts of this country is filled with meaning. The landscape that people pass through day after day contains stories that are waiting to be read.[1] The landscape in many ways is like a document that holds a wealth of information about the natural and cultural history of a place. Despite that fact, people pass through landscapes on a regular basis without gaining even a partial understanding of what that landscape is really about. How can people gain a greater understanding of the wealth of information that is available in the landscape? One way is through planned interpretation.

In recent years we have become more interested in landscape interpretation at various levels. One of the ways in which we attempt to facilitate interpretation is through the establishment of parks. We set aside physical environments for people to visit with the hope that they might gain a broader understanding of something about that environment such as its geology, ecology, or cultural history. Such parks, serve a purpose; they allow people—often in large numbers—to gain a greater understanding of the significance of a particular landscape. Those places are expensive to build and maintain. Because of that large investment, they are often intended to be "popular" and the interpretation is sometimes dedicated to flashy themes guaranteed to capture attention.

However, there remains a great deal in the larger landscape that is not interpreted. It is possible to tell a larger and more comprehensive story about the landscape than we typically do at the present time, if we expand our vision—that is get at the essence—of park. While the definition and physical description of the park has changed a number of times through history, the idea of park (the essence of park) has remained constant. It has always been about engagement and contrast, about allowing for the possibility for a mental shift to take place in the landscape. If that mental shift takes places, any landscape can be a park. If that engagement does not take place, even a place built as a park will be ineffectual. From that point of view we can think of a larger landscape as a park so long as a mental connection is made between the landscape and the mind of the human who is in that landscape. To think of the larger landscape as a park is good for people as well as the physical environment. People would be provided with numerous recreational and interpretive opportunities and even an ordinary landscape would garner greater respect.

The purpose of this paper, then, is to present to you a way of interpreting the larger historic cultural landscape (viewed as park). The benefits of this idea are many and the shortcomings are few. It will allow for interpretation even on an individual basis and at a trifling cost. It can take advantage of both public and private landscapes as they already exist and it can happen almost any where. We have selected the larger landscape near Allentown, Pennsylvania, as a test case for this idea since the National Parks Service has shown interest in interpreting that landscape.

## An Expanded Vision of Park: The Park as Idea

Parks have been a traditional vehicle for providing interpretive opportunities for people who wish to engage the landscape. But how can a park, a particular piece of geography, help us with a better understanding of the larger landscape? To answer that question we must look more closely at what the park is in essence, what the park has done for human beings for centuries. Obviously parks through history have been different kinds of places. The park began with the Assyrians as an enclosed hunting ground, a general concept that was carried forward through the centuries even past the renaissance period. In the eighteenth century with the work of Brown and Repton the park was defined as a tract of land that was designed with the new natural aesthetic that had emerged. Parks were areas of pleasure and most often included scattered groupings of trees and wide expanses of turf. By the end of the nineteenth century parks were generally considered public places, places designed for the recreational pleasure of all classes of people. Today we use the word park in many ways. There are for example ball parks, amusement parks, and of course parkways.[2]

Are there any consistent themes related to the park over time that can be derived from such a myriad of places? There are if we are willing to think beyond the park only as a place and concentrate on the park as an idea. From the Assyrian hunting park to modern day parks of all varieties the consistent themes (park as idea) are connected to the notion of recreation, being re-created. The park as an idea is about engagement and contrast; it is about a mental shift, allowing for a different connection to or understanding of the environment.[3] When that mental shift takes place the human being is rewarded in the sense that he or she is refreshed and rejuvenated as a result of that new understanding or experience. If we think of the park as an idea, then we must realize that as designers make places, the most that they can do is to provide the opportunity for a "park experience" to take place. We wish to provide the opportunity for people to be re-created and with that re-creation they might also come to a new understanding of the world they have engaged.

If we accept this understanding of park, park as the opportunity for engagement, as the opportunity for a mental shift, then we can begin to see opportunities for helping us to understand the landscape in more depth. Such an engagement is good for the observer but also for the landscape that is being observed. If we think about the landscape as a park we will perhaps interact with it in a different way than might typically be the case.

Consequently we are proposing an expanded vision of park, a vision that would remove us from the restrictions of a particular piece of geography, typically with one owner, and take us to the realm of the park as an idea. We will demonstrate that even a large landscape with several owners might be a park if it is a landscape that is carefully considered for its interpretive possibilities.

## The Historic Cultural Landscape: A Story to be Read

There are many ways to think and learn about the landscape. One can study maps or read books on the subject. But the landscape itself can reveal a great deal of information, if only we allow our selves to look (let ourselves be engaged). A story (the cultural history of the place) can be read in every landscape.[4]

The landscape of course is the result of human interaction with the natural features of the land itself. The foundation is in the underlying geology; it's physical structure and its mineral composition. In places, this foundation is staggeringly complex and hard to grasp, and in others it is uniform and comprehensible at a glance. Time and climate act upon these underpinnings and influence the specific character of the landform and the soil that covers it. Finally, communities of plants and animals inhabit the land responding to it's conditions and further interacting with them to form the natural component of the landscape.

The human contribution to the landscape is more than the playing out of history on the stage of the land—it is a further interaction. Humans shape and are shaped by the natural environment. In the process of going about the business of living their lives, people manipulate the land, alter communities of plants and animals, and build structures. They do these things not in a random way, but in response to social, political, religious and philosophical conditions.[5] Humans have always altered the landscape with the available technology; and in response to both opportunities and obstacles. The mark that people have left on the landscape—the artifacts of their lives—remain as visible landforms, distinctive patterns of vegetation, and a wide array of structures. If we can identify and interpret these artifacts, we can use them to tell the story of those people and the world in which they lived.

People live in and alter the landscape over time and as the conditions that influence their lives change the kind of artifacts that they leave change as well. Some landscapes show periods of growth and periods of stagnation, others show continuous development. In most landscapes, artifacts of different eras, or periods of time in which the conditions remain relatively stable, are overlain upon one another—each era using and adapting the landscape of the past.

When we interpret history in the landscape, we often fall into the trap of being overly selective—choosing only a subset of the artifacts in the landscape to interpret. In some cases we choose those artifacts that have the greatest design value assuming that only examples of high design are important. At other times we choose only those artifacts associated with famous people or compelling events. This selectivity assumes that there is no important history in the ordinary and that only the most enticing is worthy of interpretation.[6]

There is also more history in the landscape than can be interpreted in a collection of isolated artifacts. What makes the landscape a particularly valuable means of understanding history is that the artifacts of which it is comprised are an integral part of a landscape fabric—systems of artifacts that expand the scope of interpretation far beyond what is possible with any artifact alone.

Another form of selectivity is in the model that we often choose for historic landscape interpretation—owning, preserving, and maintaining historic sites as the basis for interpretation. These sites fit the dictionary definition of park—a tract of land set aside for public use. This definition of park as a model for interpretation is essential where structured interpretation and control over change are important. But the obvious limited resources for land acquisition and structured interpretation force us to be selective and to choose only those sites that will return the greatest amount of interpretive punch for those limited resources. Again the result is a subset of the artifacts and therefore an incomplete telling of the history of a place. How then can we interpret more of the landscape without being overly selective?

The answer lies in viewing the entire landscape as a park.

## The Concept Applied

Our goal is to provide new opportunities for people to interpret the historic cultural landscape by thinking of that larger landscape as a park. That parklike engagement is possible anywhere. Recreational and interpretive opportunities abound even in the ordinary landscape. We have selected the Lehigh Valley of eastern Pennsylvania near Allentown as an example, because the Department of Landscape Architecture at Penn State was involved in a cultural landscapes study there, because the National Park Service is interested in creatively interpreting that area, and because the Lehigh Valley contains visible evidence of over 250 years of land use that can be understood through a variety of highly interpretable themes.

One way for people to become engaged in the broader landscape is to explore it, on their own, on an interpreted driving tour. A driving tour accompanied by a well-produced guidebook provides the opportunity for people to experience the landscape first hand, have its artifacts and systems interpreted, and make the mental shift that transforms a place into a park.

What follows is a series of routes or driving tours Ð all based around a central spine. The spine allows for the interpretation of the principal themes and provides an overview of the entire region. Emanating from this spine are several loops, each designed to reveal a particular theme in the landscape in greater depth. These can be more than just driving tours however. From the car, with guide book and audio tape, the observer has the ability to see and understand historic landscapes that are privately owned. But where possible, the route should include public sites and landscapes where the observer can experience the historic landscape on foot. These could be formal interpretive facilities, walks down city streets, or parts of larger parks that contain interpretable landscapes.

## The Central Spine—The Lehigh River Corridor and the Lehigh Canal

The corridor of the Lehigh flows from the Ridge and Valley region to the north past anthracite coal fields then through the Lehigh Valley before joining with the Delaware River 50 miles north of Philadelphia. At the northern edge of the valley, the river cuts through Blue Mountain. Through the 18th and 19th centuries this water gap provided one of the few avenues of assess between the Great Valley (known locally as the Lehigh Valley) and the historically more remote mountains beyond. During the 1740s the Moravians built religious communities near the Lehigh at Bethlehem and Nazareth and by 1750 most of the Lehigh Valley was settled. After anthracite was discovered in the 1790s the Lehigh River became one of four primary corridors for transporting coal. Much of the coal made its way to Philadelphia and other destinations beyond but the Lehigh Valley itself, with rich deposits of iron ore and other minerals, became a major consumer of anthracite. The canal was built between 1818 and 1829 with the sole intent of carrying anthracite. During the 1850s railroad construction began along the Lehigh and eventually two railroads ran parallel to the canal. Because of the great volume of anthracite to be transported, the mule-powered canal was able to remain in operation and compete with the railroads into the 1920s.

Today remnants of the canal and railroad landscapes and the industries that they supported can be observed and interpreted in a relatively continuous route along the Lehigh River. Relatively intact sections of the canal remain adjacent to canal towns

## The Jim Thorpe/Summit Hill Loop—Anthracite Coal to the Canal

On the upper Lehigh, the town of Jim Thorpe (formerly Mauch Chunk) was the point where anthracite, mined on the mountain to the west, was loaded onto canal boats for transport down river. Through much of the 19th century coal was loaded onto cars at the Summit Hill mines, sent down a gravity railroad that descended 900 feet over eight miles, and then loaded onto canal boats at Mauch Chunk. The corporate headquarters of the Lehigh Coal and Navigation Company was located in Mauch Chunk and today the relative high style of the architecture reflects the prosperity that anthracite brought to the region. The gravity railroad remains as a trace on the mountain side. The towns of Summit Hill, Lansford and Nesquehoning reflect the lives of the people who worked the mines.

## The Iron Loop—Iron Mining and Production

Significant deposits of iron ore were located throughout the Lehigh Valley as well as on the slopes of the ridge to the south. The scars of ore pits and the scattered artifacts of several eras of iron manufacturing combine to tell a story of the history of the iron industry from charcoal iron in the early 19th century to the development of anthracite iron during the second half of the 19th century, to the rise and fall of the 20th century iron and steel industry at Bethlehem.

## The Slate Belt

It is easy to be struck by the abundance of slate used as a building material in and around the town of Slatington. Most of the roofs are slate Ð even barns and sheds have slate roofs. There are slate side walks, slate building foundations, and slate retaining walls. A drive through the countryside reveals slate dumps and abandoned quarries as well as an active quarry. Just as the coal in eastern Pennsylvania was metamorphosed from bituminous to anthracite with the additional pressure and temperature of being near the zone of collision between continental plates that formed the folded Appalachians, the common shale found elsewhere in the Appalachians was here turned to slate. This band of quarries, as narrow as a mile across, follows the northern edge of the Lehigh Valley on either side of the Lehigh River. Throughout much of the 19th century and into the 20th, this region was one of the few major slate producing regions of the country. The decline in the demand for slate, and the resultant stagnation of the local economy can be read in the town of Slatington itself, where there are virtually no buildings that have been built since 1900.

## Agriculture

Agriculture has been the dominant land use in the Lehigh Valley since the middle of the 18th century. Because of its extensive coverage of the landscape, agriculture is the most imageable of the historic themes in the Lehigh Valley. The Valley has two distinctly different agricultural types that relate directly to underlying geology. The more prosperous are the farms on the prime agricultural soils underlain by the Beekmantown Limestone. This landscape is open and very gently rolling. The farms are large as are the houses and barns, which are likely to be built of limestone. The other agricultural landscape is the northern part of the valley underlain by shale and slate. The topography here is more hilly and the soils are not as rich, but much of the historic agrarian landscape is nevertheless intact. It is possible the find your way very well in parts of this landscape using a map made in 1874. Because this area has seen little change during the 20th century, there are still fine examples of stone arch bridges and the older Pennsylvania German barns.

## Urban Change and Development

Urban change and development likewise has a long history in the Lehigh Valley. Change in urban fabric is more observable and can be more easily interpreted in the landscape than those in which the artifacts are less obvious. This region has a variety of specific themes of urban change that began with the old Moravian settlement at Bethlehem in the 1740s and continued through to the late 20th century edge city development near Allentown. Between are rural villages, canal towns, railroad towns, and industrial towns. In Allentown, the urban fabric itself can be interpreted to reveal 200 years of periods of growth and prosperity as well as stagnation and decline.

## Conclusion

This concept of interpreting the broader historical landscape is not intended as a replacement for either historical preservation or public parks. Instead it is presented as a supplement to those activities that allows for a more complete interpretation of history, and broader public engagement in it. Since no land would be owned or maintained as a part of the park, the cost of providing recreational and interpretive opportunities would be relatively small and dependent upon the amount of interest that was generated by the idea. The possibilities for accompanying interpretive material are many, ranging from inexpensive brochures, to books and cassette tapes, to very sophisticated high tech wizardry. An interpretive park experience of this variety is available to almost any community or geographic region. Communities, particularly those needing some economic stimulus, have nothing to loose and everything to gain as they consider ways to tell their stories holistically. Even the landscape itself has potential for gain, for the more people who understand the landscape, the less likely are they to abuse it.

## NOTES

1. See Peirce Lewis; "Taking down the velvet Rope: Cultural Geography and the Human Landscape," Ch. 1 in Jo Blattti (Ed.), *Past Meets Present: Essays about Historic Interpretation and Public Audiences.* Washington, DC: Smithsonian Institution Press; 1987.

2. Most histories of landscape architecture present the history of the park in this way—see Norman T. Newton, *Design on Land: The Development of Landscape Architecture,* Cambridge, MA: The Belknap Press of Harvard University Press, 1971; and Philip Pregill and Nancy Volkman, *Landscapes in History: Design and Planning in the Western Tradition,* New York: Van Nostrand Reinhold, 1993.

3. See Lance Neckar, "The Park: Prospect and Refuge," *Reflections,* 6, Spring 1989, pp.4-13.

4. See Lewis 1987.

5. Peirce Lewis in his contribution to the unpublished report: *Inventory and Assessment of Cultural Landscapes for the Delaware and Lehigh Navigation Canal National Heritage Coridor,* 1991.

6. See Lewis 1987.

# Early Visions for a System of Connected Parks

*Daniel Joseph Nadenicek*

## Introduction

Horace William Shaler Cleveland (1814-1900), an early pioneer in the profession of landscape architecture, designed the Minneapolis Park System in the 1880s. The design consisted of a small urban park near the center of the city that was connected by parkways to a system of parks, lakes and natural environments That park system was initially laid out far beyond the edge of the existing city providing an armature around which the city would grow for the next several decades.[1] In laying out his design in the 1880s. Cleveland prophetically encouraged community leaders to look forward a hundred years to when there would be an urban population of over a million people and Minneapolis and St. Paul had grown together. The Twin Cities Metropolitan Area did grow as Cleveland predicted and the park system he designed is today considered one of the best in the country.[2]

What was the origin of that idea for a system of urban parks? Historians often have treated Frederick Law Olmsted's Emerald Necklace design for Boston as the prototypical connected system that later influenced the work of a number of individuals including Cleveland. However, Cleveland considered the idea of connecting parks long before Olmsted began his Boston work in the late 1870s. In fact, the seed of the idea was sown and began to germinate even prior to the design Central Park. The story of the development of the idea of a system of connected parks is complex.[3] The development of that concept—as is so often the case in history—was a result of an evolutionary process, which can be traced at least back to the mid-1850s.

It was an idea that was also connected to important literary explorations by prominent American writers about the landscape and civilization.[4] It is no accident that the founders of the profession were first writers before they became landscape architects. Cleveland and his partner Robert Morris Copeland (1830-74), were particularly influenced by the thought and writing of the Transcendentalist leader, Ralph Waldo Emerson. Those early landscape architects tested Emerson's aesthetic principles in the real landscape in 1855 with the design of Sleepy Hollow Cemetery, Concord, Massachusetts. Sleepy Hollow was more than a cemetery; it was designed as a park and was an integral part of a system of public open space, a town-country continuum.[5] Copeland and Cleveland were also influenced by Emerson's "organic aesthetic," which in landscape art meant a close connection to the integrity of the found landscape and a disdain for artificial embellishment.[6]

From the design of Sleepy Hollow forward Cleveland and Copeland were leaders in the evolutionary development of the idea of connecting urban parks.[7] The name Emerald Necklace, often associated with the Boston Park System, is a misnomer in the sense that it is sometimes presented as a metaphoric title befitting Olmsted's master stroke of creative genius. However, a careful reading of Zaitzevsky coupled with a comprehensive understanding of the careers of Cleveland, Copeland, and Copeland's protege, Ernest Bowditch, reveals the true story of the Boston's System; it was an idea that began to evolve in the minds of community leaders and designers as early as 1856.⁸

## A New Profession: Scientific Farming and Literature to Physical Design

The development of the idea of connected parks cannot be separated from the development of the profession of landscape architecture in the United States by the mid-nineteenth century. Cleveland and Copeland were both scientific farmers and writers before they began their career as landscape designers.⁹ Cleveland was a scientific farmer in New Jersey beginning in the early 1840s. and Copeland followed suite in Massachusetts about ten years later. Scientific farmers were concerned with the practical and the utilitarian, but they were also interested in aesthetics.¹⁰

They believed that their experiments and writing on the subject would work to elevate the American farmer (and therefore a significant percentage of the American populace) physically, mentally and morally. Copeland was so convinced of the importance of this task that he wrote an eight hundred page guide on agriculture and landscape gardening titled *Country Life*. Copeland began that book with the following words:

> To all lovers of nature and to all engaged in cultivating and adorning the earth, this book is dedicated, with the earnest hope that it may attract to the practice of the arts of culture some who will see that the pursuit is full of pleasure, . . . and also with the hope that some who now earn their bread with the sweat of their brow, . . . will learn that within the round of their daily duties they have every thing which can expand the mind and ennoble the soul.¹¹

By the 1850s agricultural and horticultural experimentation and writing about the affective potential of the landscape was a common pursuit of many well-to-do New Englanders, professional writers, and active farmers such as Cleveland and Copeland.¹² Those individuals shared their ideas in print—especially in such publications as the *New England* Farmer. When in 1854 Copeland and Cleveland formed a partnership to provide services in landscape and ornamental gardening and agricultural engineering (they included scientific farming services along with design services), they relied on their literary and scientific farming connections to gain work. In 1854 Simon Brown, the editor of the *New England Farmer* and Concord resident, enlisted Copeland's advice for the design of the State Farm at Westborough, Massachusetts.¹³ In 1855 Copeland participated in the Concord Lyceum Series, organized by Brown and Emerson. He delivered an address about art, architecture, and landscape gardening entitled "The Useful and the Beautiful." In the same year the Concord, Massachusetts Cemetery Committee, which included Emerson as a member, retained the services of Copeland and Cleveland to design Sleepy Hollow Cemetery. Sleepy Hollow Cemetery is the final resting place of Emerson, Nathaniel Hawthorne and Henry David Thoreau, but it is also a built reflection of a number of Emerson's aesthetic ideas. Cleveland and Copeland not only had a personal and professional relationship with the Transcendental leader, they also studied his work and were influenced by many of his ideas.¹⁴

## Emerson's Vision and Influence

Emerson influenced the future work of Copeland and Cleveland in two ways. First his writing about aesthetics guided their practice throughout their entire careers. Second, Emerson's vision of civilization and urban life directly influenced their real experiments in urban design. In his writing Emerson promoted an organic aesthetic for all of the arts. He believed that art should be true to that which is found in nature and he had a strong disgust for artificial embellishment. He also believed that the development of details of any work must be accomplished "so that the whole presents a union of [the] integrated parts."[15] The idea of being true to place and connecting the parts to the whole was a driving impetus in all of the work of Copeland and Cleveland.

Emerson also wrote a great deal about a particular vision of civilization and urban life. Though urban experience was often in direct opposition to any natural experience, Emerson believed—unlike his Romantic counterparts in Europe—that some reconciliation of those two worlds was not only possible, it was necessary for the future of American civilization. As Michael Cowan, a leading scholar on Emerson's urban theories has written:

First, he [Emerson] wished to see the physical city become more creatively related to its natural hinterland and more internally "natural" or "organic." Second, he wanted to find ways by which the poet [artist, even artist in the landscape] might integrate the growing industrial city into an artistic work that professed to embody organic principles.[16]

Nature, believed Emerson, if carefully planned for in the design of cities could stimulate the spiritual and moral development of human beings and augment the creative role of civilization.

Emerson worked with these ideas in a direct and straight forward way in his home community of Concord, Massachusetts. He was always able to balance the dual roles of distant sage and practical community leader. From the 1830s forward, he made himself available to the affairs of Concord. One of his important contributions was his service on various committees concerned with the public grounds of the community.

The concern for the larger landscape of Concord was at first related to the need for more burial space. The office of the Superintendent of Public Grounds was organized in the late 1840s to address that and other needs of the community and Emerson's friend John Keyes filled that position for the first several years. It was as a result of recommendations from Keyes, Emerson, and others that the town acquired the plot known as Sleepy Hollow in the early 1850s. The site had been known as Sleepy Hollow for more than twenty years and it is likely that it was given that name because it reminded citizens of Irving's picturesque descriptions of its New York namesake in the "Legend of Sleepy Hollow." On September 29, 1855 Emerson delivered his "Address to the Inhabitants of Concord at the Consecration of Sleepy Hollow" in which he explained the design, the design intent, and the aesthetic vision for the cemetery.

Sleepy Hollow was designed in keeping with Emerson's organic aesthetic. It was gracefully fit into a natural amphitheater and a number of native species were planted in the landscape. As if in answer to Emerson's calling the designers sought to be true to the place. In that landscape those that visited the graves of friends and relatives could be sure that indeed even human beings are part of the "vast circulations of nature."[17] In addition to its obvious function as a final resting place, the cemetery was also meant to serve the Concord community as a public park, where citizens might come together for games, civic functions, and education.[18] "The acquisition and design of Sleepy Hollow represents forward thinking in another way ... the community leaders [including Emerson] perhaps in consultation with Copeland and Cleveland, began thinking about a system of public open space that extended from the heart of the community to Sleepy Hollow and beyond."[19]

Sleepy Hollow, said Emerson, "fortunately lies adjoining to the Agricultural Society's ground, to the New Burial Ground, to the Court House and Town House, making together a large block of public ground, permanent property of town and country—all the ornaments of either adding so much value to all."[20] As early as 1855, inspired by Emerson, Copeland and Cleveland considered the possibility of connecting one community, Concord, with their interpretation of the natural environment on the fringe.

## The Truth About Boston

In truth the design for a system of connected parks for Boston began at about the same time as Sleepy Hollow. In 1856 Copeland and Cleveland offered suggestions for the design of Commonwealth Avenue in Boston. As Boston's back bay was being filled, a number of individuals became concerned with the planning and the dispersal of lots on that plot of land. Under the Commonwealth of Massachusetts Resolves of 1856 a committee, comprised of members of the state house and senate and local commissioners, was organized to deal with issues related to the new lands. It was to this committee that Copeland and Cleveland offered their suggestions for the design of Commonwealth Avenue.[21] Copeland and Cleveland advised the committee that the width of the proposed avenue should be increased from 170 to 240 feet allowing for a large middle portion that might be planted with rows of trees and used for the recreational enjoyment of citizens which "would be ample for walks and seats secure from the interference of carriages."[22] The avenue from the beginning of Copeland and Cleveland's involvement was viewed as a parkway (or boulevard) that might connect the Common and Public Garden in Boston with other areas for recreation on the periphery. It was with that purpose in mind—perhaps following the suggestions of Copeland and Cleveland—that the committee wrote:

> It is believed that an ornamental avenue of this character, . . . with stately dwelling-houses upon each side, connecting the public parks in the centre of a busy city with attractive and quiet, although populous country in the neighborhood, is a thing not possible of construction elsewhere in the world; and those places where some thing of the same kind already exists have been rendered famous in the consequence.[23]

The filling of the back bay made Emerson's vision of the city possible for Boston. As early as the 1850s, a number of individuals including Copeland and Cleveland, were in the process of contemplating the physical possibilities of that idea. Even prior to the beginning of the Civil War the concept of a connected park system for the greater Boston area was in the early stages of its evolutionary development. Emerson's Aesthetic vision as translated by Copeland and Cleveland and the actual filling of the back bay contributed to that possibility.

The development of that idea like much in American civilization was waylaid by the Civil War. However, soon after the end of the war those issues were again revisited. Copeland and Cleveland continued to refine their thinking during the late 1860s. It is clear that by 1868 the idea of a system of connected parks had reached a higher level of sophistication in the minds of designers and community leaders alike. Copeland had studied the idea in considerable depth. The pivotal year in the history of the evolution of urban park systems appears to be 1869. In "The Public Grounds of Chicago: How to Give Them Character and Expression," written in that year, Horace Cleveland considered future parks for a number of cities with special emphasis on Boston and Chicago. Cleveland wrote "If Boston attempts a park comprising any attractions of natural scenery, she must go beyond her own limits."[24] Also in 1869 Copeland wrote an article for the *Boston Daily Advertiser* in which he outlined his scheme for a municipal and metropolitan park system of great magnitude. By 1872 he had distilled and fine tuned his thinking to the point that he was able to publish a pamphlet entitled "The Most Beautiful City in America: Essay and Plan for the Improvement of the City of Boston." In that tract Copeland argued that Boston needed a number of smaller parks and public open spaces rather than a large central park such as in New York. Though Copeland's scheme was far from perfect, he did considered a number of areas—such as the Fens and part of West Roxbury—which ultimately become part of the final plan for the Boston system.

Just as Central Park was preceded by an extensive editorial campaign, a connected park system for Boston was promoted in editorials for years before it became a physical reality. Many of the editorials related to that idea in the early 1870s were written by Copeland. Of course, it did not hurt that his brother-in-law, Charles F. Dunbar, was the editor of the *Boston Daily Advertiser* during the 1870s. Copeland used that newspaper as a soapbox from which to expound on the benefits of such a system for the citizens of Boston. In one of those articles Copeland spoke of a parkway that would thread its way through parks "of several places instead of one, the selection to be in different parts of the future and present city."[25] The idea of a park system for Boston was developed and heavily promoted by Copeland and others in newspaper editorials and articles prior to Copeland's death in 1874.

It was also during early 1870s that Copeland employed a young engineer named Ernest W. Bowditch. Bowditch was educated in engineering at MIT. For a time he worked for the office of Shed and Sawyer, Engineers. Copeland hired the services of that office on many occasions during the 1870s, since they were located in the same building as Copeland. Copeland worked directly with the young Shedd and Sawyer apprentice, Ernest Bowditch, on a number of projects. When Copeland felt that he was being over charged by Shedd and Sawyer, he persuaded Bowditch to split off from that office and set up an office of his own. Copeland offered Bowditch a considerable amount of work as an incentive for that change. Bowditch, at the time in his early twenties, was more than willing to take the plunge. Immediately, Copeland and Bowditch began to cultivate a close working relationship that functioned much like a loose partnership. It was during that period (from 1872 to 1874) that Bowditch was introduced to Copeland's scheme (which Copeland was continuing to refine) for a connected park system for Boston. In March of 1874 Copeland died unexpectedly. The following excerpt from Copeland's obituary, probably written by Dunbar, reveals that the idea of a park system was foremost in his mind at the time of his death. "He had done much in the way of laying out and ornamenting private grounds, but his ambition was for work on a grander scale."[26]

Bowditch seized what he perceived to be a great opportunity and purchased Copeland's practice in landscape architecture. He formed a partnership with Copeland's brother Franklin, believing that the Copeland name would bring him business and add credibility to his practice. On June 24, 1874 Bowditch published an article and plan for a Boston park system in the *Advertiser*. Since Copeland was known to have been working on the scheme at the time of his death and because Bowditch was a twenty-four year old engineer with little experience in landscape architecture, it is likely that Bowditch in the article was really presenting Copeland's work (with perhaps only minor changes). He had probably waited for an adequate amount of time to pass after Copeland's death before presenting that work to the public.[27]

But Bowditch was a quick study and proved to be a capable student of landscape design. He continued to refine and improve the scheme which he had inherited. In 1875 Bowditch published another pamphlet for public consumption titled "Rural Parks for Boston."[28] That publication included a plan that showed a remarkable similarity to the park system plan presented to the public by the Boston Park Commission in 1876.

## The Idea Taken West

It is clear that in 1876 Olmsted had only a sketchy understanding of the entire system at best.[29] He had only been tangentially connected to the development of the idea for Boston. On the other hand, in fairness, it must be said that during the same years Olmsted was considering similar ideas for other cities such as Buffalo. But that work should be seen only as part of the overall evolutionary process. In fact, all of the early landscape architects discussed in this paper communicated with one another about the idea on a regular basis. Copeland, for example, presented the concept in a letter to Olmsted already in 1869 asking him to comment.[30] Cleveland worked for Olmsted on Prospect Park before he headed west in 1869 and no doubt the two men conversed about the concept. Cleveland once in Chicago immediately set out to test the idea in built environments in the Midwest.

Prior to 1870 he laid out the community of Highland Park, Illinois where he designed a parkway leading from the heart of the community out to a natural ravine area near the edge. The 1870s was a difficult period for Cleveland's practice. His office burned in the "Great Chicago Fire" of 1871 and he suffered a loss of business as a result of the financial panic of 1873.[31]

The idea of organization new cities around a connected park system was ultimately put into place by Cleveland in Omaha and Minneapolis. Cleveland began promoting the general concept for the Minneapolis system already in the 1870s, but it was not until the 1880s when the milling town appeared to be destined for unharnessed growth that Cleveland was finally given his chance. The Minneapolis Connected Park System was the crowning achievement of Cleveland's long career and it provided the armature around which the city would grow for the next several decades. There he was able to take ideas that he began to glean from Emerson as early as the 1850s and apply them in a new and burgeoning western city.

## ACKNOWLEDGMENT

This research was funded in part by a grant from the Institute for the Arts and Humanistic Studies, Penn State.

## NOTES

1. H. W. S. Cleveland, *Suggestions for a System of Parks and Parkways for the City of Minneapolis*. Minneapolis: Johnson, Smith & Harrison, 1883, pp. 3-15.
2. Lance M. Neckar, *Fast-Tracking Culture and Landscape*. An Unpublished Paper. Minneapolis: University of Minnesota, 1990, pp. 17-18.
3. The story is even more complex if one factors in a number of developments in Europe related to the idea of connecting various public open spaces in urban environments. Though Americans were influenced by developments in such places as Vienna and Paris, the discussion of that work is beyond the scope of this paper.
4. I first became interested in the significance of literary ideas to the early development of landscape architecture while writing my MLA thesis at the University of Minnesota which was ultimately titled The Literary Landscape of Horace Cleveland. Also see Daniel Joseph Nadenicek, "Nature in the City: Horace Cleveland's Aesthetic" forthcoming in a special issue of Landscape and Urban Planning.
5. See Daniel Joseph Nadenicek, "Sleepy Hollow Cemetery: Transcendental Garden and Community Park," forthcoming in *The Journal of the New England Garden History Society*.
6. Michael H. Cowan, *City of the West: Emerson, America, and Urban Metaphor*. New Haven, CT: Yale University Press, 1967, pp. 184-85.
7. This is true except for that small interlude in American History commonly known as the Civil War.
8. Cynthia Zaitzevsky, of course, wrote Frederick Law Olmsted and the Boston Park System. The purpose of this article is not to diminish the accomplishments of Olmsted, his work in the Fens for example will always stand as preeminent achievement in design. But the idea of a connected system for Boston must be seen as it is, the result an evolutionary process.
9. Obviously the same is true of Olmsted. In fact at the time that Cleveland and Copeland began their practice Olmsted was still engaging in scientific farming experiments at his home on Staten Island.
10. Nadenicek, "Cleveland's Aesthetic."
11. R. Morris Copeland, *Country Life: A Handbook of Agriculture, Horticulture, and Landscape Gardening*. Boston: John P. Jewett and Company, 1859, p. ii.
12. Included among the writers who were interested in this realm was Ralph Waldo Emerson who raised pears and studied the natural environment and even his own garden.
13. Simon Brown Journals at the Concord Antiquarian Museum, Concord, MA.
14. Emerson knew Copeland well enough that he was willing to serve as a character witness for him in the 1860s. Cleveland wrote of Emerson in letters to friends and "The Aesthetic Development of the United Cities of St. Paul and Minneapolis." I have recently had an article accepted for publication in the Emerson Society Papers about Emerson's aesthetic influence on Cleveland.
15. Vivian C. Hopkins, *Spires of Form: A Study of Emerson's Aesthetic Theory*. Cambridge: Harvard University Press, 1951, pp. 66- 80.
16. Cowan, *City of the West*, p. 183.
17. Ralph Waldo Emerson, "Address to the Inhabitants of Concord at the Consecration of Sleepy Hollow," *Emerson Papers*. Cambridge: Houghton Library, Harvard University, Sept., 1855.
18. Ibid., part of the educational experience was connected to an arboretum planted in the cemetery.
19. Nadenicek, "Sleepy Hollow Cemetery."
20. Emerson, "Consecration Address."
21. Walter Muir Whitehall, *Boston: A Topographic History*. Cambridge: Belknap Press of Harvard University Press, 1968, p. 151. Also working on the scheme was the architect Arthur Gilman. That information can also be found in "Report of the Committee Appointed Under the Resolves of 1856," Ch. 76, in *Relation to Lands in the Back Bay with Accompanying Documents*.
22. "Resolves," p. 14.
23. "Resolves," pp. 14-15.
24. H. W. S. Cleveland, *The Public Grounds of Chicago: How To Give Them Character and Expression*. Chicago: Charles D. Lakey, Publisher, 1869, p. 8.
25. News article in the *Boston Daily Advertiser* dated October 24, 1873. Though the article was unsigned, it was almost certainly written by Copeland. Zaitzevsky comes to that conclusion as well.
26. Copeland's obituary in the March 30, 1874, *Boston Daily Advertiser*.

27. Cynthia Zaitzevsky, *Frederick Law Olmsted and the Boston Park System.* Cambridge: The Belknap Press of Harvard University Press, 1982, p. 41.
28. "Reminiscences of Ernest W. Bowditch," The Essex Institute
29. Ibid., p. 43.
30. Ibid., p. 36.
31. Cleveland continued to refine the idea of connected public spaces despite that downturn. He worked with the idea in the design of a number of "romantic suburbs" and he modeled the concept in the design of a cemetery in his home town of Lancaster, Massachusetts, in 1873. The design of that cemetery should be seen as a model for Cleveland's concept of urban growth and connected environments. The cemetery was laid out like a city with a dense area of stones and ornamental plantings at the center. From there the density of grave sites decreased dramatically as they moved out toward the edge of the forty acre site. Cleveland also designed three distinct groves in which those scattered graves were set. The groves were in keeping with the integrity of the native landscape. The dense urban core was connected to the natural groves by a long tree-lined avenue or parkway.

# Managing the Blue Ridge Parkway Viewshed: A National Forest Perspective

*Terry Seyden*

I have enjoyed a long personal relationship with the BRP. I've told Gary Everhart that my wife and spent our honeymoon at Pisgah Inn 19 years ago. What I didn't say, was that we only stayed there because I got high fever on a backcountry Forest Service trail, and the Pisgah Inn was the closest available motel.

More recently we have spent six years in Roanoke and two years in Asheville, and both times have lived within a mile or two of the Blue Ridge Parkway. Our family has spent many enjoyable hours at places like Peaks of the Otter and Pisgah Inn.

In my position of public affairs officer, I get to deal with many controversies and public issues; National Forest timber management within sight of the Blue Ridge Parkway has gotten its share of my attention over the years.

I will talk today of how the Forest Service manages the scenic values of the national forest land that you see while driving along the BRP.

The Forest Service and the Blue Ridge Parkway have a long tradition of working together. The National Forests in North Carolina were created out of lands that nobody wanted. Logging between the late 1800s and early 1900s, in many places, left a sea of stumps and badly eroded land.

The Pisgah National Forest was founded in 1914 with the first land coming from the original holdings of the Biltmore Vanderbilt Estate. The BRP was created in the 1930s, in many cases with land transferred from the National Forests.

Nearly 200 miles of the parkway goes through four national forests in Virginia and North Carolina. When you are driving along the parkway, many times you are looking out onto national forest lands.

The backbone of how the national forests protect scenery is our visual quality objective system. Each National Forest is zoned according to the relative visual sensitivity of the area. Visual quality objectives (VQOs) vary from preservation in the most sensitive areas such as wilderness, to retention, partial retention, modification, and maximum modification. All of these terms refer to the amount of visual disturbance that is allowed to *occur*

Critical viewpoints from roads and trails are identified and different VQOs are assigned depending on the overall management objectives for that part of the forest and how much visitor use occurs in that area. Another factor we consider is how far away the activity is from a particular sensitive viewpoint.

We divide distance into three zones: The foreground includes everything up to half mile away. The mid ground ranges from 1/2 mile to 2 miles distant, and background is defined as three or more miles away.

In North Carolina, we recently met with Jim Ryan and parkway officials recently to go over our long range forest planning maps. A lot of national forest land that is in the foreground or midground distance zone as seen from the Blue Ridge Parkway is now out of what we refer to as our suitable timber base so no commercial timber harvest activity is planned. In those areas visible from the parkway that are still in the timber base, we will manage the foreground (up to 1/2 mile away) to fully retain the area's current visual appearance, and we will manage the midground (1/2 mile to 2 miles distant) to at least partially retain the area's current visual appearance.

Let's look at some examples of what activities that we would consider as meeting various levels of visual quality.

- Preservation
- Retention
- Partial retention
- Modification

   (Several slides were shown depicting recent activities that meet the following visual quality objectives. Copies of example slides available upon request.)

In retention and partial retention areas it is our intention that we will meet the assigned VQO after one full growing season. One question we often get from our district people is whether this VQO has to be met during the summer when the trees have their leaves on, or also in the winter when the leaves are off and you can generally see farther and notice a lot more evidence of man's activities. We take the stricter approach and say that the VQOs must also be met during the leaf off winter season, even though this is a time when there are a lot few visitors on the forest or the parkway.

Managing the viewshed is more than leaving a thin chlorophyll curtain along roadways and playing peekaboo with our clearcuts. Today harvest methods are changing on the National Forests across the south, and especially in those areas which are the most visually sensitive, like the Blue Ridge Parkway and Appalachian Trail.

In recent times the Forest Service relied heavily on a harvest method called clearcutting. Clearcutting is a method in which all the merchantable trees are removed from an area up to 25 acres in size, and the site is then prepared for establishing a new stand of trees. Clearcutting is an efficient method and has proven to be an effective way of regenerating valuable tree species such as oaks. However, clearcutting if done improperly and in the wrong locations can be downright ugly.

We are now developing a number of alternatives to clearcutting. The Forest Service now has a new policy in which clearcutting will be used only when other harvest methods are inappropriate or not feasible.

Roads are sometimes our biggest visual concern. Long after the trees have grown back the roads will still be visible. We are addressing this by building low standard, temporary roads wherever possible and quickly revegetating the road bed with grasses and in some cases shrubs and trees. But if the road is on a permanent location and will be used again, chances are that you will be able to see the roadway for many years.

Of course, as we have all heard, beauty is in the eyes of the beholder. Public complaints from parkway visitors have been few, and cut over tree stands in this part of the country grow back very quickly. When a timber harvest unit is over 20 years old, it takes a trained eye to pick it out from the surrounding forest. A recent VPI study found that people most prefer viewing an unbroken canopy of trees in the distance. Other studies show that many people enjoy a greater visual variety, including some vistas and naturally appearing openings in the forest viewshed.

Your perspective also makes a difference. A small clearcut used to open up a scenic vista along a road side would get no complaints, while most would find that same opening objectionable if it were perched on a sideslope that you are staring directly toward.

Also, complicating matters is the steep topography which often requires us to use cable equipment to extract the timber products. However, these Southern Appalachian forests contain northern red oak and other high quality hardwoods that are highly prized for use in making fine furniture.

There are no absolute right or wrong answers here. It is more a question of accurately understanding and responding to public values, which can change over time. We place a high premium on maintaining the beauty of national forests and are willing to forgo some timber values to maintain the scenic quality of the forest as seen from the parkway.

Let's talk some now about the mechanics of how we coordinate our timber sale program with the BRP. Several years ago, we informally coordinated with the parkway, but occasionally something fell through cracks. Sometimes Parkway field people were OK with our proposed projects, but Gary and company in Asheville were a little more demanding. Also, in a few cases some timber cuts turned out to be more visible than we anticipated.

In 1988, the Forest Service and the Blue Ridge Parkway signed an interagency agreement, which called for early and frequent coordination, field trips, and BRP staff review of Forest Service timber plans before final decisions were made. Through perspective plots and other computerized techniques we can see ahead of time what proposed harvests will look like.

The new long range management plan for the Nantahala and Pisgah National Forests in North Carolina will place a premium on visual quality. Similar to other forests in southern Appalachians, we are moving away from clearcutting. Instead of clearcutting, the Forest Service is making greater use of group selection and two aged harvest methods.

In group selection, we harvest small groups of trees an acre or two at a time. While being less efficient, these smaller openings are much less noticeable to the average forest visitor or tourist who is looking out onto the forest while driving the Blue Ridge Parkway.

The other harvest method we are using is a modified shelterwood that we refer to as two aged management. Typically we will harvest only a little more than half of the mature trees in any given stand, and leave the remaining tress for a long period of time, thus creating a forest stand that has two distinct age classes of trees.

The advantage of this approach is that you provide a greater variety of wildlife habitats and these types of cuts are much less visible at a distance to the casual parkway or forest visitor. In fact we have several examples of these two age harvests that are within several miles of the Pisgah Inn. Because of the screening provided by the remaining uncut trees, it is almost impossible to pick out the units, even in the winter with the leaves off the trees

Here in the National Forests in North Carolina we receive over 30 million visitors a year, by some estimates more than the Smokies and BRP combined. The National Forests in North Carolina has a multiple use mission. We maintain healthy forest ecosystems and provide habitats for a wide variety of plant and animal species. We offer valuable wood products, but at the same time we are committed to managing a forest that is attractive and pleasant to visit.

# Design and Construction of Park and Waterway Bridges

*Eugene C. Figg, Jr.*

## ABSTRACT

The design of bridges in park and waterway environments requires design and construction solutions that protect the environment and develop harmony with bridge and environment. The presentation of case studies of successful bridge projects in park and waterway environments demonstrates consideration of aesthetic components and leads to the development of a comprehensive design philosophy. The design philosophy outlines six themes that are used to evaluate bridge aesthetics. The result of incorporating the design philosophy is bridge designs that are environmentally sensitive to construct, serve their users, have pleasing aesthetics, and are in harmony with their environment.

## INTRODUCTION

Bridges in park and waterway environments present unique engineering challenges. The bridge designer must develop bridge design and construction solutions guided by two principles:

- Design and construction solutions that protect the environment.
- Design and material solutions that are in harmony with the environment.

Figg Engineering Group's experience includes many projects through sensitive environments of parks and waterway areas, as well as other environments where bridge aesthetics are of critical importance. Case studies are presented herein which describe our experience in the design and construction of park and waterway bridges. Through these case studies, the aspects of design and construction that serve to protect the environment and harmonize with the environment are discussed. In addition to these case studies, Figg Engineering Group's design philosophy used to ensure overall aesthetics of a bridge project is presented. Specific examples supporting this philosophy or design approach are presented and discussed.

## DESIGN AND CONSTRUCTION SOLUTIONS THAT PROTECT THE ENVIRONMENT

Many innovative design and construction methods for precast segmental concrete bridges have been used to build America's most environmentally sensitive bridges. The ability to precast concrete segments of the substructure and superstructure of the bridge off-site greatly reduces impacts to the natural environment. In addition, precast concrete box girders offer construction techniques that can be built from the top, such as balanced cantilever with an overhead gantry or one directional, progressive cantilever. These construction schemes can be tailored to the bridge site to preserve the natural environment in very sensitive areas like parks and waterways. Two such projects are the *Linn Cove Viaduct* in North Carolina and the *Hanging Lake Viaduct* in Colorado. These two bridges were successful because construction schemes allowed them to be built from the top, above environmentally sensitive terrains. Further discussion of these two projects will illustrate how bridges can be built over rugged terrain through parklike environments using innovative construction techniques.

*Linn Cove Viaduct, North Carolina—* The viaduct in North Carolina represented the last major link in the completion of the last seven (7) miles of the 469-mile Blue Ridge Parkway, which connects two national parks—Shenandoah and Great Smoky Mountains. This picturesque eastern U.S. area has attracted millions of Americans and international visitors since the 1930s, when construction of the Parkway first began.

For more than 10 years the Federal Highway Administration (FHWA) searched for a construction method for the viaduct that would not harm the scenic beauty of the Parkway, owned by the National Park Service (NPS). The FHWA decided that a segmental bridge was the best solution. The FHWA determined the location of the bridge, established design criteria, performed the foundation investigation and design, and was responsible for overall construction administration. In a team effort with the FHWA, the consultant provided the technical staff to prepare the bridge design and assist in construction of the segmental portion of the bridge.

*The Linn Cove Viaduct is* a curved, post-tensioned precast concrete box girder bridge, 1,243' long, built from the top down. There are eight (8) spans: 98.6'-163'-4 @ 180'-163'-98.6'. The viaduct hugs the contours of privately owned Grandfather Mountain, but only the piers touch the mountain. The bridge seems almost suspended in space, offering unparalleled vistas of the Blue Ridge Mountains.

Erected by progressive placement in one-directional cantilever, the Linn Cove Viaduct is the only bridge in North America to be erected by this method. The Linn Cove site had limited access—only one way in and out—and the progressive placement method allowed the delivery of segments, equipment and construction materials over the completed portion of the bridge from a single access point. It also provided easy access to all pier locations, enabling each pier (also built in precast segmental) to be built as the superstructure reached that point. The bridge piers are an octagonal shape with curvilinear faces that form shadow lines and provide improved aesthetics. During the entire construction progress, in order to maintain the "park concept" of the Parkway, stringent environmental constraints were met: no trees were cut, other than those which physically occupied the same space as the bridge, and no rock outcroppings were damaged.

Precast segmental bridge construction and the construction scheme selected provided the most economical solution to meet all the environmental requirements. The precast method also allowed casting to continue during the severe winters experienced at this elevation. All the reinforcing cages were prefabricated and all the segments were cast inside a building erected by the contractor about two miles from the bridge site.

Because of its vertical and horizontal alignment and site constraints, the Linn Cove Viaduct is one of the most complicated bridges ever built. The horizontal alignment includes spiral curves transitioning to circular curves with radii as small as 250' and with curvature in two directions, which gives the bridge its distinctive "S" shape. Only a small portion of the bridge is on a horizontal tangent. The super-elevation of the roadway goes from a full 10% in one direction to a full 10% in the other direction and partway back again within the length of the bridge. The viaduct includes every kind of alignment geometry used in highway construction.

No two of its 153 superstructure segments have the same dimensions, and only one the segments in the entire bridge is straight. The nominal dimensions for the segments are 8'-6"10 long, 37'-6" wide, and 9' deep. Segments were match-cast using the short-line system. Only one casting machine was used for casting of the superstructure segments. The complex geometry of the bridge was established by the relationship between segments in the casting machine. The sharp curvature results in extreme angular deviations between the two match-cast segments; this required a casting machine that had hydraulic adjustments at all four corners.

A specialized geometry control system was required during the casting operations. The Figg Engineering Group computer programs transformed field coordinates of the final bridge to a coordinate system compatible with the casting machine, in order to facilitate verification of the contractor's as-cast geometry. These programs also incorporated the structural deformation data supplied by the Bridge Construction (BC) bridge design program used in the design of Linn Cove. The measurements were taken to an accuracy of .001 ft. The system placed the control points exactly at the joints and corrected for all movements which could possibly occur during casting. No segments were rejected during the entire construction.

Aesthetics were paramount to the National Park Service. The segments for the viaduct were cast using one of the most sophisticated concrete mixes ever developed for a segmental bridge in the U.S. The coarse aggregate was crushed dolomitic stone, and the fine aggregate was quartz sand. Admixtures included air entraining agents, retarders, and a super water reducer. To achieve the aesthetics desired by the NPS, an iron oxide pigment was also added to tint the concrete mix to match exactly the color of the existing rock on Grandfather Mountain. As a result, the completed viaduct looks as if it has always been a part of the face of Grandfather Mountain, blending harmoniously with the ancient rock.

*Hanging Lake Viaduct, Colorado*— The Hanging Lake Viaduct, in Glenwood Canyon, Colorado, completes one of the final remaining links to the original Interstate highway system.

The project site is located within an extremely steep and narrow portion of an environmentally sensitive canyon. Pressure from both the general public and public agencies dictated that the design of the highway through the canyon blend with the sensitive environment and not disturb the canyon's natural beauty. The bridges were built using precast segmental box girder construction, which allowed the design to meet the owner's strict requirements for overhead erection, aesthetics, and construction schedule.

The project consists of two structures totaling approximately 8,400 linear feet of bridge with typical span lengths of 200'. The east-bound structure is 1,308' long and the west-bound bridge follows the steep, rocky talus canyon slopes for 7,121'. Both structures emerge from twin tunnel portals and cross the Colorado River with 300' spans. The west-bound bridge also ends in a tunnel portal at the east end of the project.

One of the project's requirements was for the structure to blend as much as possible with the natural beauty of the environment. This was accomplished by using longer spans (200') to minimize the number of piers along the over-one-mile-long viaduct structure. The structure depth was also kept to a minimum for the span length used. A constant depth section was used to better blend with the natural predominant horizontal lines of the canyon rock walls.

The horizontal and vertical alignment of the bridge was designed to minimize the impact, both physically and visually, to the canyon. The horizontal alignment follows the natural contour of the canyon and river to provide a smooth, flowing ribbon through the canyon, again blending with the natural surroundings. The vertical alignment rises to 80' above the existing roadway to clear all trees and natural slopes below the structure.

The Hanging Lake area of the canyon has long been viewed as a special and unique section by all parties due to the magnificent sheet rock walls and the popular Hanging Lake Trailhead and rest area. The views from the trailhead were determined to be the most critical of the entire canyon. Therefore, as part of the agreement to build the project, the highway would cross the Colorado River just upstream of the trailhead and enter a tunnel to bypass and hide the highway from this critical scenic and recreational area.

Since the river crossing would become part of the view shed from the trailhead, the aesthetics of this particular span were of prime importance. The owners wanted a relatively long span over the river for both aesthetic and constructibility reasons. Pier construction in the river would be costly due to the deep layer of soft clay and muck in this part of the canyon. Also, due to the relatively low vertical clearance of the alignment over the river and the natural horizontal lines in the canyon walls, a thin, constant depth structure was thought to look best for the span. A 300-foot span was selected due to the span appearing "centered" over the river when viewed from the trailhead area.

As mentioned above, the nominal span length selected for the longer viaduct section of the project was 200 feet based on both aesthetics and constructibility issues. The optimum girder depth determined for this span length was a constant 10 feet.

Aesthetically and economically for precasting, the optimum solution for the 300 foot span was continuing the 10 foot section over the river. However, structurally this was not feasible and as a compromise, a special variable depth section was developed to obtain the necessary additional structural depth. By decreasing the slope of webs in the variable depth area to .75 :1 from the typical web slope of 4:1, the effect of a constant depth section could be achieved due to the created shadows. The constant depth line is further enhanced by a horizontal offset of three inches at the bottom web corner. The width of the deepened section at the pier matches the transverse and longitudinal faces of the typical canyon elongated octagonal shaped pier, adding to the aesthetic qualities of the detail.

The precast, post-tensioned box girder section provided the flexibility that allowed these pleasing proportions, curves, and aesthetic details to be an economical structural solution as well. The final aesthetic touch to the structure is the application of a colored concrete coating to further enhance the bridge's harmony with its natural surroundings.

As previously mentioned, public pressure required that the bridges be built without disturbing the sensitive environment. In addition, there are no reasonable alternate routes capable of handling the interstate traffic at either end of the canyon and, therefore, maintenance of traffic during construction was equally important to the owner as preserving the environment. Thus, the owner required the design of the structure to be such that the superstructure be entirely erected from the top without the use of ground-based equipment which would interfere with traffic or disturb the environment. Also prohibited was the use of falsework or temporary bents during construction in areas where traffic or the environment would be affected.

Given these construction requirements, the concrete alternate was designed using precast box girder segments erected in balanced cantilever entirely from the top using an overhead launching gantry. The segments were trucked over the completed section of bridge and then placed alternately in cantilever to either side of the pier using the gantry. The gantry was self-launching and could be advanced from the previous cantilever to the following pier without additional ground or structure based equipment. The 300' mainspans were designed with a temporary bent in the river to allow a gantry designed for 200' spans to be used to erect the longer span.

The project was bid in 1989 and awarded to the low bidder of $34 million, including 5,000' of roadway construction, and $1 million lower than the alternate steel box girder design. The entire project was opened to traffic in October, 1992.

The precast segments were held in place with post-tensioning bars and every other segment in the cantilever also anchors multi-strand cantilever post-tensioning tendons. After casting a closure joint in place to connect the cantilever tips, bottom slab tendons were stressed to provide the positive moment capacity of the span.

The precast segmental erection method not only allowed the Contractor to meet the project's tight construction schedule, but to finish erection five months early. This allowed the owner to open the structure to traffic early as well, and again help minimize the inconvenience and delays for the traveling public through the heavily traveled canyon. The Contractor was able to average completion of approximately one 200' span per week during the erection of the long west-bound structure. This was possible due to the advantages of precasting the segments year round, thus giving the Contractor the option to accelerate the erection schedule during the longer summer days.

The superstructure is constructed with precast box girder segments. The typical section is 34'-6" wide, 10' deep and 8' long. The segments were cast at a precasting plant approximately 20 miles from the bridge site which has been in operation for over 10 years. The casting plant has three typical casting beds and one special bed for diaphragm segments such as pier, abutment and expansion joint segments. To meet the project schedule, segments were cast year round inside buildings. A total of 1,156 segments were cast for the project.

The segments varied in weight from 38 tons to 46 tons and were stored at the casting yard until ready for shipment to the bridge site by truck. Prior to shipment, the segment decks were post-tensioned transversely at the plant.

## DESIGN AND MATERIAL SOLUTIONS THAT ARE IN HARMONY WITH THE ENVIRONMENT

Bridge design involves the scientific work of engineers based on the structural analysis to select, proportion, and detail the features of the bridge to meet the structure's required function. Even though this work is of a technical nature, it also involves a degree of artistic and aesthetic consideration. In bringing art and science together, the challenge is to simultaneously develop forms that follow function while producing structures with pleasing aesthetics. Figg Engineering Group's comprehensive design philosophy works to incorporate both the scientific and the artistic elements of design. The six building blocks or themes of this philosophy are:

- Focus on concrete bridge designs.
- Configure bridge layouts to open

vistas and invite user participation.
- Select functional, pleasing bridge shapes that consider the human dimension.
- Incorporate native materials.
- Accent bridge colors and texture.
- Incorporate lighting solutions to highlight bridge features.

## Concrete Bridge Designs

Concrete box girder bridge designs offer smooth surfaces of continuous flat planes. This continuity of surfaces offers significant aesthetic opportunities. While a trapezoidal box girder cross-section provides an appearance that is neat and simple, when properly designed it produces an efficient and cost effective structure as well. The long term durability of prestressed concrete serves to reduce maintenance costs and provide cost savings throughout the service life of the structure. The aesthetic benefits, cross-section efficiency, and low life cycle cost are all reasons to focus on concrete as the material of choice when designing bridges for park and waterway environments.

## Bridge Layouts

Figg Engineering Group's design philosophy features bridge layouts that both open new vistas to the users and follow natural terrains. Structures such as the *Linn Cove Viaduct* and the *Natchez Trace Parkway Arches* offer motorists views of landscapes that were not available prior to the construction of these facilities. The *Natchez Trace Parkway Arches* will be the first precast segmental arch bridge in America with a principal arch span of 582 feet.

While these structures open up park areas for the enjoyment of the motorists, the structure must also be designed so it does not dominate the landscape. Horizontal alignments, vertical profiles, and super-elevations were selected for these bridges to skirt mountain sides and dip through valleys, marrying the bridges to their sites.

## Shapes

The third theme of the Figg Engineering Group design philosophy is the selection of functional, pleasing bridge shapes that consider the human dimension. These considerations range from selecting dimensions of the superstructure cross-section to selecting the overall shape of the entire bridge that will be seen in a silhouette. The shape of the superstructure is most effected by the structure depth and the angle at which the webs slope. The structural depth (and therefore span lengths) must be selected to give the structure a light and smooth flowing, graceful appearance. The *Dauphin Island Bridge* in Mobile, Alabama consists of 118' long approach spans with a 7' deep box girder cross-section. To accommodate the 400' mainspan and maintain unity with the structure the superstructure depth varies from 7' to 22-1/2' at the pier. A circular intrados was used for ease of construction and for its aesthetic appeal.

The *Escatawpa River Bridge* near Mosspoint, Mississippi with a 300' mainspan, utilizes straight haunches to increase the structural depth at the piers. Most often with variable depth box girders with inclined webs a reduction in the bottom soffit width occurs from the span centerline to the pier locations. This is not especially advantageous from either a structural or aesthetic viewpoint. The *Escatawpa River Bridge*, however, maintains the width of the bottom soffit of the variable depth box girder and varies the inclination of the sloped webs. The constant width bottom soffit allows a better flow of stresses in the box girder section and does not detract from the structure's aesthetic appeal.

While the variable depth cross-section is the logical approach to providing added moment capacity at pier locations, there are situations where a variable depth cross-section is not desirable. Such was the case with the *Hanging Lake Viaduct*. As previously discussed, for aesthetic reasons a constant depth superstructure was needed to help the structure blend in with the striated canyon walls. This required the design of a special detail at the main pier locations which allowed for a variable depth cross-section for the 300' mainspan across the Colorado River but gave the appearance of a constant depth cross-section to blend with the canyon walls.

**Native Materials**

Native materials should be incorporated when practical. This further brings the bridge together with its setting. Native materials were used in the construction of the *Linn Cove Viaduct* in North Carolina. Native stone facings were applied to the base of the piers and the abutments to help this bridge blend with the mountain terrain.

Similarly, the *Wiscassett Bridge* over Maine's Sheepscot River utilizes granite facings on the piers. The granite facings were used to minimize the "highwater" mark on the piers due to the extremely high tidal fluctuation and to help the structure blend with the environment. Granite was also used for the curbs.

The *Pimmit Run Bridge* on the George Washington Parkway near Washington, DC represents the use of native materials for a bridge rehabilitation. This was a re-decking project for a steel girder bridge with a concrete deck. The re-decking scheme allowed for the use of precast concrete panels which were ultimately post-tensioned transversely and longitudinally. While the truly significant feature of this project is the fact that the structure could be re-decked in only five (5) weekends without disruption to rush hour traffic, an added aesthetic benefit was gained by the use of stoneclad curbs and abutment walls. This allowed the rehabilitated bridge to blend with the other features of the parkway setting.

**Colors and Textures**

Closely related to the use of native materials is the fifth theme of the Figg Engineering Group's design philosophy—use of colors and textures to accent a bridge structure. This is most often used in the case of urban bridges where the bridge structure exists in well traveled areas. An example where colored texture was applied to a bridge in a parklike setting is the 1-110 *Biloxi Bridge* in Biloxi, Mississippi. This bridge is built through very limited right-of-way and traverses a residential area. By using precast concrete box girders, the area underneath the structure benefits from the smooth flowing lines of the superstructure. This results in an area that is usable as a "commons" area for local residents. By applying a colored texture coating the area is even further enhanced. With the addition of walking paths, lamp posts, and landscaping, the area under this bridge serves the area residents as a recreational area.

The *Linn Cove Viaduct* also utilized color to enhance the structure's aesthetics as previously discussed. Iron oxide (found in the natural rock outcropping on Grandfather Mountain) was added to the concrete mixture to tint the concrete. The color match between the concrete and the rock outcroppings added harmony between bridge and mountain.

Another example of using color is the *Brandywine Creek Bridge* in Delaware. This bridge is presently under design and as part of the design process, concrete colors and tints have been examined that might be used to match the stones and boulders in Brandywine Creek and surrounding area of the bridge. This will help the proposed structure blend in with the natural environment.

**Lighting Solutions**

The last aspect of the design philosophy is the incorporation of lighting solutions to highlight the bridge features. An example of where lighting was used effectively is the *Sunshine Skyway Bridge* in Tampa, Florida. The cable-stayed structure has a 1,200' mainspan. With the cable-stays painted gold the lighting gives the bridge a dynamic impact at night. In a park or waterway setting, bridge lighting can also be used to light areas below the structure to also serve as security lighting.

## CONCLUSION

Through the use of these six themes or building blocks of the Figg Engineering Group design philosophy we have been able to design bridges that are environmentally sensitive to construct, serve the users, and are in harmony with their environment. The consideration of bridge aesthetics should be at the heart of the design of all bridges, and in fact, aesthetics can not be separated from good bridge design. *America Deserves Beautiful Bridges.*

# The Appalachian Trail Crosses the Cumberland Valley
## A Case Study of Corridor in Response to Cultural Landscape Preservation, Agricultural Preservation, and Landscape Ecology
Neil P. Korostoff and Tom Yahner

### Abstract

The Appalachian Trail is a pedestrian hiking facility of some 2,000 miles running through the Appalachian Mountains from Maine to Georgia. It was originally conceived by Benton McKaye (then of the Regional Planning Association of America) in 1921 as a plan for revitalizing a depressed region via a program of contiguous natural reserves fro recreational activities and development of silvicultural and agricultural resources. This development was largely unrealized though the trail itself has been established through public and private land holdings.

The U.S. Department of the Interior, through the National Park Service (NPS), has recently begun purchasing land along the length of the Appalachian Trail to secure public ownership of this important facility. Passing predominantly through forested ridge and valley terrain, the trail makes its longest valley crossing in Pennsylvania where the 16-mile-wide Great (Cumberland) Valley, an intensively cultivated area, lies between two forested ridges. The NPS has acquired a corridor for the trail which consists of a low, wooded, ridge across a limestone valley and agricultural land typical of the Pennsylvania cultural region. It crosses two streams, major highways and local roads. Adjacent to the trail corridor, agricultural land is rapidly giving way to suburban development and transportation facilities. The corridor land is managed by the Cumberland Valley Appalachian Trail Management Committee (CVATMC), a local arm of the Appalachian Trail Conference. The CVATMC sought the assistance of the Landscape Architecture Department at the Pennsylvania State University to develop a design and management plan for the trail and corridor.

The goals of the design and management plan for the trail corridor across the Cumberland Valley include developing a hiking experience that derives its character from the natural and cultural features of the local landscape; stewardship of the ecological, cultural, and cultural resources within the corridor; establishment of an ecological corridor linking the nearby forested ridges; and coordination of land use, recreation, and conservation planning with adjacent townships. This paper presents this project as a case study in corridor design and planning in response to cultural landscape preservation, agricultural preservation, and landscape ecology.

---

Contact authors at the Department of Landscape Architecture, Penn State University, University Park, PA 16805; telephone 814-863-2377.

# Congress and the Establishment of the John D. Rockefeller Jr. Memorial Parkway, 1971-1972

*Philip A. Grant, Jr.*

On February 9, 1972, Republican Senator Clifford P. Hansen of Wyoming introduced a bill to establish the John D. Rockefeller Jr. Memorial Parkway. According to the terms of Hansen's bill, the proposed parkway would link Yellowstone and Grand Teton National Parks in Wyoming and would be administered by the National Park Service. Approval of the parkway had been strongly recommended on February 7, 1972, by Secretary of the Interior Rogers Morton.[1]

A former governor of Wyoming, Hansen in 1972 was completing his first of two terms in the U.S. Senate. Hansen was a member of the Senate Committee on Interior and Insular Affairs and the ranking Republican serving on its Subcommittee on Parks and Recreation.[2]

On the date he offered the John D. Rockefeller Parkway Bill, Hansen delivered an address in the Senate chamber, the object of which was to provide colleagues with a brief explanation of the provisions of the measure. Hansen maintained that it was important that the NPS exercise jurisdiction over the parkway "in order that it may be protected from any future activity that would detract from its natural beauty. The Wyoming Senator concluded that the "designation of this area as the John D. Rockefeller Parkway would offer the kind of protection necessary to preserve this magnificent area."[3]

The Hansen Bill was promptly referred to the Interior and Insular Affairs Committee, a panel consisting of nine Democrats and seven Republicans. After scrutinizing the bill for six weeks, the committee on March 22, 1972, issued a unanimous report in favor of its passage.[4]

Considered to be noncontroversial in nature, the John D. Rockefeller Parkway Bill was brought to the Senate floor on March 25. Without any discussion, the Senate routinely approved the bill by a voice vote.[5]

On February 17, 1972, a bill, largely similar to the Hansen measure, was introduced in the House of Representatives by Congressman John P. Saylor of Pennsylvania. Saylor was the ranking Republican member of both the House Committee on Interior and Insular Affairs and its Subcommittee on the Environment. Serving his twelfth of thirteen terms in the House, Saylor had established himself as one of the foremost proponents of conservation on Capitol Hill.[6]

The Saylor Bill, as expected, was submitted to the 39-member Interior and Insular Affairs Committee. It was not until more than five months later that the committee reached a decision on the bill. On July 25, the committee issued a favorable report on the bill, noting that it differed somewhat in its specifics from the Hansen Bill.[7]

The John D. Rockefeller Jr. Memorial Parkway Bill was brought to the House floor on August 14. Urging passage of the measure were Congressmen Saylor, Roy A. Taylor of North Carolina, and Wayne N. Aspinall of Colorado. Taylor and Aspinall respectively chaired the Parks and Recreation Subcommittee and the Interior and Insular Affairs Committee.[8]

Saylor emphasized that the parkway "would directly benefit visitors to the two national parks by providing a continuity of service and protection." Please that the parkway would link together two of the country's "most outstanding national parks," Taylor noted that the bill was designed "to protect the scenic and recreational values of the area immediately adjacent and intimately associated with these two parklands." Aspinall, hailing the Rockefeller Parkway Bill as "sound legislation," concluded that the bill would "improve the efficiency of the administration of the entire area" and would "insure the future integrity of the connecting corridor for the benefit and enjoyment of the public."[9]

After less than ten minutes of perfunctory discussion, the House assented to the Rockefeller Parkway Bill without the formality of a roll call. Since there were slight differences in the language of the Senate and House bills, there was a distinct possibility that it might be necessary to appoint a conference committee to reconcile a few items. On August 17, the Senate simply agreed to concur with the text of the House bill, and eight days later President Nixon formally signed the bill into law.[10]

In its final version the John D. Rockefeller Jr. Memorial Parkway Act consisted of four sections. Section One authorized the Secretary of the Interior to establish the parkway, to make minor revisions in its boundaries with the concurrence of the Secretary of Agriculture, and to administer the existing and future connecting roadways. Section Two stipulated that the Secretary of the Interior could acquire land from another federal agency "by donation, purchase, exchange, or transfer" and from the State of Wyoming "only by donation." Section Three permitted hunting and fishing "in accordance with the applicable laws of the United States and the State of Wyoming" and decreed that lands within the parkway were "hereby withdrawn from location, entry, and paten under the United States mining laws." Section Four placed a limitation of $25,000 for the acquisition of land and imposed a ceiling of $3,092,000 for the overall development of the parkway.[11]

The John D. Rockefeller Jr. Memorial Parkway Bill was one of the 6,042 bills offered for consideration throughout the duration of the Second Session of the Ninety-Third Congress. After its enactment by the House and Senate, it became one of the 383 public laws of 1972.

The JDRMP was the logical culmination of the sequence of events which began with the establishment of Yellowstone National Park in 1872, the passage of the NPS Act of 1916, and the creation of the Grand Teton National Park in 1929. It also became the country's fourth national parkway, joining the George Washington Memorial Parkway of 1930, the Blue Ridge Parkway of 1936, and the Natchez Trace Parkway of 1938.[12]

The JDRMP differed somewhat from the three earlier parkways in the eastern half of the U.S. The George Washington Memorial Parkway became primarily a commuter thoroughfare along the Potomac River across from Washington, D.C. The Blue Ridge Parkway, extending from the Shenandoah National Park in Virginia to the Great Smoky Mountain National Park in North Carolina, was 477 miles long. The Natchez Trace Parkway, located in Tennessee, Alabama, and Mississippi, was 447 miles long. By contrast, the JDRMP was only 82 miles long and was in the midst of a remote section of one of the nation's most sparsely populated states.

While the JDRMP Bill was initiated by two Republican congressmen, Senator Hansen and Representative Saylor, the bill enjoyed broad bipartisan support in the Senate and House Committees on Interior and Insular Affairs. Also facilitating its passage were the endorsements by Wyoming's two Democrats on Capitol Hill,

Senator Gale W. McGee and Representative Teno Roncalio.[13]

In terms of cost, the JDRMP Bill was a rather modest proposal. While the bill limited expenditures for the parkway to $3,117,000, an examination of the congressional appropriations for 1972 established that the parkway accounted for only a small fraction of the money approved for the NPS and the Department of the Interior. In 1972, Congress appropriated $221,133,000 for the NPS and $2,548,935,000 for the Department of the Interior.[14]

## NOTES

1. U.S. Senate, *S. 3159-A Bill to Authorize the Secretary of the Interior to Establish the John D. Rockefeller Jr. Memorial Parkway*, and for other purposes, February 9, 1972; Robert Sobel, ed., *Biographical Directory of the United States Executive Branch, 1774-1989*, Westport, CT: Greenwood Press, 1989, p. 272.

2. Bruce A. Ragsdale and Kathryn A. Jacob, eds. *Biographical Directory of the American Congress, 1774-1989*, Washington, DC: GPO, 1989, p. 1128; Robert Sobel and John Raimo, eds, *Biographical Directory of the Governors of the United States, 1789-1978* (4 vols.), Westport, CT: Meckler Books, 1978, vol. 4, p. 1783; U.S. Congress, *Congressional Directory, 1972*, Washington, DC: GPO, 1972, pp. 198, 263.

3. U.S. Congress, *Congressional Record*, Washington, DC: GPO, 1972, vol. 118, pp. 3327-3329.

4. U.S. Senate, *Report Number 707*, March 22, 1972; *Post*, Washington, DC, March 16, 1972, p. 33; *New York Times*, March 19, 1972, p. 62.

5. *Congressional Record*, vol. 118, pp. 10112-10113.

6. U.S. House of Representatives, *H.R. 13201-A Bill to Authorize the Secretary of the Interior to establish the John D. Rockefeller Jr. Memorial Parkway, and for other purposes*, February 17, 1972; *Congressional Record*, vol. 118, pp. 4342-4343; *Biographical Directory of the American Congress*, p. 1772; *Congressional Directory, 1972*, pp. 157, 284; *The Almanac of American Politics, 1972*, Boston: Gambit, 1972, pp. 716-717.

7. U.S. House of Representatives, *Report Number 1237*, July 27, 1972.

8. *Biographical Directory of American Congress*, pp. 552, 1918; *Almanac of American Politics, 1972*, pp. 120-121, 603-604.

9. *Congressional Record*, vol. 118, pp. 28100-28103.

10. *Congressional Record*, vol. 118, pp. 28633, 29192, 29303, 29807.

11. *The Statutes at Large of the United States of American, 1972*, Washington: GPO, 1973, vol. 86, pp. 619-620.

12. *Statues at Large*, vol. 17, pp. 32-33; vol. 39, pp. 535-536; vol. 45, pp. 1314-1315; vol. 46, pp. 484-485; vol. 49, p. 2041; vol. 52, pp. 407-498 [sic]; Hiram M. Chittenden, *The Yellowstone National Park*, Norman, OK: U. of Oklahoma Press, 1964; Philip A. Grant, "Congress and the Development of the Natchez Trace Parkway, 1934-1946," *Parkways: Past, Present, and Future, Proceedings of the Second Biennial Linear Parks Conference, 1987*, Boone, NC: Appalachian Consortium Press, 1989, pp. 156-162; Harley E. Jolley, *The Blue Ridge Parkway*, Knoxville: U. of Tennessee Press, 1969.

13. *Congressional Record*, vol 188, pp. 5727, 15434; *Biographical Directory of American Congress*, pp. 1464, 1740.

14. *Statutes at Large*, vol. 86, pp. 508-525; *Congressional Quarterly Almanac, 1972*, Washington, DC: Congressional Quarterly, Inc., 1973, pp. 516-520.

# Beauty and the Beast: Locational Logic of the Blue Ridge Parkway

*Lisle S. Mitchell*

This presentation intends to validate the "Beauty and the Beast" metaphor for the marriage of the Blue Ridge Mountains to the Parkway; to explain the geographer's concern and interest in the parkway and in the location of its recreation facilities; to discuss the theoretical logic of positioning recreation facilities along a leisure travel path; to compare the actual configurations of recreation facilities with the theoretical arrangement using a nearest neighbor technique; and to summarize the findings of this research project and discuss the need for additional research.

## Beauty and the Beast as Metaphor

As a father of a nine-year-old and the grandfather of a four-year-old, I have been intimately aware of *Beauty and the Beast* as a book and as a movie. Even before its relatively recent popularity, I have long been aware of the fairy tale, the Broadway play, and the television series. When I was first made aware of the theme of this conference, "Marrying Beauty With Utility," I immediately thought of the "Beauty and the Beast" metaphor, or analogy, for the marriage of the functional, cultural roadway (i.e., the Beast) to the scenic, natural Blue Ridge (i.e., Beauty).

While "Beauty and the Beast" imagery is entirely subjective, it is easy to relate to the beastly man-made construction marring the beautiful natural mountainscape. The Blue Ridge Parkway includes several areas where forms of construction and transport routes through the mountainous regions are less than charming. Still, there are areas which highlight the successful merger of the unmatched beauty of the undulating and meandering topography of the Blue Ridge with the roadway. The Linn Cove Viaduct is one of a number of views of the parkway which seem to validate the triumph of such a union.

## Geographic Concern

To the public, geographers seem most concerned with naming countries and their capitals or with the leading resource, agricultural, manufacturing, and handicraft commodities of the fifty states. Few geographers hold such encyclopedic knowledge high on their priority lists. Broadly, geographers' concerns are categorized in four general topics: 1) earth science or the comprehension of the natural phenomena and processes found on the earth, 2) cultural environmental relationships or the examination of human interaction with the resources of the earth, 3) area studies or describing the nature and character of a specific portion of the earth, such as a country, and 4) a spatial or aerial perspective primarily concerned with why things are located where they are on the earth's surface.

In studying the relationship of the Blue Ridge Parkway to the natural environment, this research is concerned with both area studies and spatial studies, examining the distribution of twelve recreation facilities along the parkway. Is there logic or rationale to explain the spacing of recreation sites along a 470-mile stretch of wildly wandering and rolling roadway? The geographer assumes everything found on the earth's surface can be explained. What is seemingly distributed by chance is simply not understood clearly enough yet to be explained. The inquiring mind of a geographer is bent on investigating such

Figure 1. Theoretical Distributions and Nearest Neighbor Analyses

**Concentrated (R=0.0)**
- tunnels (R=0.55)

**Random (R=1.0)**
- easels or interpretive signs (R=0.88)
- parking areas or overlooks (R=1.01)
- road access (R=1.14)
- trail access (R=0.96)

**Uniform (R=2.0)**
- campgrounds (R=0.95)
- gift shops (R=1.22)
- lodging (R=0.88)
- picnic tables (R=1.01)
- restaurants (R=1.17)
- service stations (R=1.04)
- visitor centers (R=1.02)

---

phenomena until the understanding comes.

## Theoretical Distributions

Research on the distribution of recreation phenomena along a leisure travelway is limited. In fact, I know of no studies that have examined the spacing of leisure facilities along a roadway built solely for recreation. There are expected or theoretical patterns of how certain kinds of facilities should or ought to be configured along a line. Theoretically, points along a line may take on three configurations: concentrated, uniform, or random (Figure 1). A perfectly concentrated pattern consists of a single point located at any position along a line. A uniform schema has a number of points equally spaced along a line. A random pattern has not discernible, visual, or statistical pattern of distribution.

Tunnels are the only facilities of the twelve recreation facilities found along the Blue Ridge Parkway that have concentrated patterns. Tunnels on the parkway should have an agglomerated distribution because they are located on the southwest end of the parkway in an area of extremely rugged natural topography. A number of man-made facilities should have a relatively uniform distribution as an efficient means of serving the needs of the traveling public. Facilities with uniform distribution include campgrounds, gift shops, lodging, picnic tables, restaurants, service stations, and visitor centers. Randomly distributed facilities include easels or interpretive signs, parking areas and overlooks, road and trail accesses. All of these facilities are specifically related to the randomness of the natural features to which they provide access or reference.

## Nearest Neighbor Analysis

Methods of examining points along a leisure travel path are limited to visual inspection, a method that is extremely unreliable, and linear nearest neighbor procedures. There are a number of such techniques, but only one is used in this research. In nearest neighbor measurements, the linear distance between adjacent locations of each facility type must be found. Fortunately, the data were readily available in *The Blue Ridge Parkway Log*, a source for all roadway facilities along the parkway by tenths of a mile. With this information, the necessary data was easily gathered to test the null hypotheses that all of the facilities are not significantly different from a random distribution. The specific linear nearest neighbor method used was devised by Pinder and Witherwick (1975) and provides a single statistical value describing the distribution. This statistic, represented by "R," is calculated by dividing the theoretical distance between nearest neighbor facilities and the actual or observed distance. A perfectly concentrated distribution would have a value of 0.0, and absolute random configuration would be 1.0, and an ideal uniform pattern would be 2.0. Of course, in the real world, nothing is perfect and a significance test is used to determine if values between 0.0 and 1.0 and between 1.0 and 2.0 are statistically different from random.

Of the twelve recreation facilities, only tunnels were expected to have a concentrated distribution and this was found to be the case. The theoretically expected distance for tunnels was 10.66 miles; the observed distance was 5.87 and the R-value was 0.55. In this case 0.55 was found to be statistically different from 1.0, and therefore the distribution of tunnels along the parkway tends to have a clustered or concentrated pattern. This finding was expected because of the rugged topography located at the southwest end of the parkway's route.

Nearest neighbor statistics for recreation facilities with random distributions due to their unpredictable locations are shown in Figure 1 in actual R-values. The R-values range between 0.88 and 1.14, none of which are significantly different from 1.0 or random. These findings were not unexpected as there is no rational reason to expect other distributions nor is there evidence in the literature to suggest otherwise.

Campgrounds, gift shops, lodging, picnic tables, restaurants, service stations, and visitor centers were expected to have layouts that approached uniformity. Regular spacing was anticipated because of the service they provide travelers. It was surprising, therefore, when all of the nearest neighbor statistics were found to be random instead (Figure 2). The R-values ranged from 0.88 to 1.22, and several (e.g., restaurants and gift shops) were very close to having a statistical tendency to be uniformly distributed. It was even more surprising to find that campgrounds and lodging had R-values less than 1.0 and had aerial patterns slightly more concentrated than random, when it was expected they would have been more uniform than random. Historically, these findings are surprising because of the lack of commercial development adjacent to, but off of, the parkway in the years immediately following construction. Currently, the random distribution does not seem illogical, because of the large-scale development of services provided in close proximity to the parkway.

## Summary and Conclusion

Of the twelve patterns of recreation facilities located along the Blue Ridge Parkway, only five conformed to theoretical expectations. The seven facilities in unexpected configurations were all service facilities found in random distribution. Since these services are currently provided elsewhere nearby the parkway, the irregular arrangement on the parkways proves not to be a serious anomaly. In the past, however, such an arrangement would not have efficiently met the needs of travelers.

The genius of the planners and engineers shaping a ribbon of concrete along a dramatically undulating and wildly meandering ridge line, while preserving and enhancing the beauty of the natural and cultural landscape is apparent even to the casual observer. The intuitive logic of positioning facilities along the roadway for the traveler is not so clearly seen. In spite of this, the original design was spatially sound and had resulted in a nearly perfect marriage between Beauty and the Beast.

Attempts to verify the random findings of the nearest neighbor analyses presented have not been successful using different methods. It is the objective of this geographer to continue the search into the locational logic of the Blue Ridge Parkway.

www.ingramcontent.com/pod-product-compliance
Lightning Source LLC
Chambersburg PA
CBHW031153160426
43193CB00008B/352